Polygamy: A Very Short Introduction

T0016974

Very Short Introductions available now:

Available soon:

For more information visit our website

www.oup.com/vsi/

Sarah M. S. Pearsall

POLYGAMY

A Very Short Introduction

OXFORD
UNIVERSITY PRESS

OXFORD
UNIVERSITY PRESS

Oxford University Press is a department of the University of Oxford.
It furthers the University's objective of excellence in research, scholarship,
and education by publishing worldwide. Oxford is a registered trade mark of
Oxford University Press in the UK and certain other countries.

Published in the United States of America by Oxford University Press
198 Madison Avenue, New York, NY 10016, United States of America.

Library of Congress Cataloging-in-Publication Data

Names: Pearsall, Sarah M. S., author.
Title: Polygamy : a very short introduction / Sarah M.S. Pearsall.
Description: New York, NY : Oxford University Press, [2022] |
Series: Very short introduction | Includes bibliographical references and index.
Identifiers: LCCN 2021033933 | ISBN 9780197533178 (paperback) |
ISBN 9780197533192 (epub)
Subjects: LCSH: Polygamy—History.
Classification: LCC HQ981 .P34 2022 | DDC 306.84/2309—dc23
LC record available at https://lccn.loc.gov/2021033933

1 3 5 7 9 8 6 4 2

Printed in Great Britain by
Ashford Colour Press Ltd., Gosport, Hants., on acid-free paper

To Amy

Contents

List of illustrations

Acknowledgments

Here are my very short acknowledgments. With characteristic generosity, Andrew Graybill and Ari Kelman encouraged me to write this Very Short Introduction and shared their terrific proposal. (I will politely forebear mentioning that my VSI is appearing before theirs.) Helpful comments from Margaret Jacobs, Andrew Preston (whose inspirational VSI fortunately did come out before mine), and especially Andrew Arsan much improved an earlier draft, as did insightful and engaged reports from anonymous reviewers for Oxford University Press. Nancy Toff has been an excellent editor, and I appreciate all she and everyone at OUP have done here. All errors remain my responsibility.

Writing this book during a global pandemic has been a challenging enterprise. I thank the staff at Cambridge University Library, who worked to strengthen electronic holdings and who implemented and managed a Click and Collect book borrowing service that proved invaluable. I am also grateful to Gary Gerstle, the Mellon Fund, and the Cambridge University History Faculty for helping me to purchase books so I could carry on with the research and writing. I much appreciate sustaining support from Teddy Kail as well as Mark Johnson.

The dedication is to my exceptional friend, Amy Gambrill, a world traveler who immediately understood why polygamy was important. Thanks for that, and much more.

Introduction

Has marriage traditionally been only one man plus one woman? Of course not. For much of human history, over most of the globe, the most common alternative to this model was polygamy—marriage involving more than two spouses. Polygamy, or plural marriage, has been an accepted form of union in the majority of human societies, among every major world religion. People living on every continent have practiced this form of marriage; some still do. Plural marriages, like more recent same-sex marriages, offer intriguing access to the workings of the institution of marriage, as well as the controversies linking public and private, sex and politics, that have surrounded it.

The story of this marriage form is a political history, not simply a social or domestic one. Marriage, whether monogamous or polygamous, has been a central way of organizing power across human history. Marriage defines family life, rendering certain relationships legitimate and allowing for inheritance and the distribution of property. For rulers across human history, marriages, including plural ones, have had particular significance, legitimating offspring, strengthening kingdoms, and ensuring takeovers. More broadly, defining some marriages as civilized and progressive and some as backward and barbaric has staked out a set of claims about the superiority of some people over others, with implications for race, religion, economics, culture, and society.

1

This process excluded certain kinds of people from a wider nation or community. Putting these boundaries in place took centuries, even millennia, and involved people around the globe. Ideas about polygamy and what it means reveal much, not only about gender but also about race, nation, and civilization itself. This topic can seem marginal, but in fact it is powerfully significant, even if we do not always think about it. Indeed, the silent, embedded nature of what I have elsewhere called "the infrastructure of monogamy" shapes our worlds in ways we do not always appreciate.

People in the early twenty-first century often think of polygamy in one of two ways: as either pious, prairie-dress-clad Mormon wives in the American West or a Turkish harem, with half-naked women guarded by eunuchs. Two pictures from the 1880s United States—one a photo of an actual Utah family, the other a whiskey advertisement—encapsulate these stereotypes. The former is a product of the nineteenth century, and the other goes back several centuries earlier. Neither captures the rich and variegated history of global polygamy. Still, these reductive images matter because they have informed all kinds of accounts and assertions. They have even influenced laws, as when the US Supreme Court ruled against allowing plural marriages in the United States in 1879, declaring that "polygamy ... was almost exclusively a feature of the life of Asiatic and of African people." Europeans and Americans have over centuries cast polygamy as an inferior form of marriage, one that indicates the problematic nature of certain people. They thus tied domestic organization to political, cultural, and racial categories.

Polygamy has a complex politics, within as well as beyond households. Confrontations over this type of marriage have been historically significant, especially in a range of colonial, imperial, and missionary encounters. They have influenced contacts between different peoples; moreover, they have provoked debates within particular cultures and countries. Although polygamy

1. A husband and his six wives show how they were living the Principle of plural marriage in Utah Territory in the 1880s, at the height of federal attempts to end polygamy in the territory. Although their garb is dark and sober, each wife's dress is distinctive.

could seem like a problematic form of marriage, even amid Christians, it has had notable defenders, including a number of radical Protestants such as John Milton, the author of *Paradise Lost*, and Joseph Smith, the founder of the Church of Jesus Christ of Latter-day Saints (Mormonism).

It is not always easy to define or even to identify polygamy, and there have been various kinds. Most have been forms of polygyny, a husband with more than one wife, although there are occasional practices of polyandry, one wife with many husbands. Nearly all global instances of polygamy involve polygyny, not polyandry. One of the few notable exceptions occurs among some modern Himalayan people, among whom a woman, in marrying an eldest brother, is considered to have married all his brothers. Polygamy includes both forms, but in practice, it has mostly been polygyny. There is no single monolithic polygamy. The term itself has been contested, with a preference in some contexts for plural marriage

2. This American whiskey ad from the 1880s exploited long-standing if mistaken stereotypes of the sensuality and debauchery of the Turkish harem, with one presumed eunuch presiding over a room full of semiclad women. The connection between whiskey and the harem is left to the viewer's imagination.

or, in the case of Mormons, celestial marriage or "the Principle." The word polygamy is used here partly to indicate that it is an imagined system, as much as a lived reality, and for ease of reference. Still, each society's practices of plural marriage differed, and they were dynamic, changing systems.

Moreover, the line between married and not married has not always been clear to communities or even to individual households, and there have been forms of union not recognized by law. There have been temporary or short-term secondary marriages, contracted for a set amount of time, which have sometimes been sources of controversy. Centuries ago, a Wendat man in northeastern North America could marry a woman with full ritual; she became his *atenonha*, or wife. In addition, he could contract a short-term marriage with a woman who became his *asqua*, or concubine. Conflict has often attended different definitions of who was married, and communities have not always been aligned with what the state saw as a marriage. For instance, the law did not recognize the marriages of enslaved individuals in anglophone colonies in mainland North America and the Caribbean, yet even masters and mistresses identified "husbands" and "wives" among enslaved people, as did some churches. So, it is not always easy to make clear who is married, whether in monogamy or in polygamy.

This book focuses on situations of public, legal polygamy in which the spouses knew about each other, rather than what one anthropologist has called "de facto polygamy," or the countless examples of someone having multiple sexual or romantic partners or keeping secret wives in different places or what we might call serial monogamy. These situations have occurred in virtually every society; what concerns us here is something more particular, defined by law. Admittedly, it is impossible to draw the lines entirely clearly, especially for earlier eras. As supporters of polygamy have pointed out, men in particular have often had multiple sexual partners, but polygamy, unlike adultery or fornication, confers the benefits of legal marriage, as well as the public status of a wife with rights to support and inheritance, on the women involved. In addition, it legitimates any children of the union.

The history of polygamy connects with the history of divorce. Some Catholics in particular have considered marriage with legal divorce and remarriage a form of serial polygamy, equally deserving of condemnation. Some proponents of polygamy advocated for divorce as well, seeing both as a way to circumvent unhappy marriages. The focus here is on formal polygamy, publicly practiced. There has been considerable diversity, but the practice of polygyny has often had certain unifying themes.

First, polygamy reveals a great deal about gender and its operations. Marriage has fundamentally ordered what women and men do and the roles they have. It is more obvious what men have historically obtained through polygamy: access to women and their sexual, reproductive, and productive labor. It brings more children, building a man's kin connections. It thus supports patriarchy and men's public importance, as well as their domestic potency. For women, the advantages of polygamy can be harder to see, and certainly some situations of polygamy have offered few. The mere fact that most polygamy has been polygyny suggests the profound and ubiquitous gender imbalances it entails. Some situations have allowed women to gain status as especially senior wives of powerful men. In some forms of polygamy, wives could share child care and household labor. Women, too, could benefit from a wider range of kin connections. Women have used polygyny to limit births, as a husband has more children but each plural wife has fewer. In eras before reliable birth control—that is, most of human history—birth limitation could offer an advantage for women. This book considers, as much as possible, the perspectives of the wives who lived polygamy, though this is not always easy to do because they left far fewer firsthand accounts, especially in earlier periods.

Sex and reproduction form a second major theme. The classic image, as the whiskey ad suggests, is that men enjoy the access to multiple women's bodies that polygyny provides; in some cases, they have. However, too much focus on this aspect obscures what polygamy does in terms of reproduction. Polygamy has worked in tandem with populations keen to build themselves up, whether in ancient Israel or in the nineteenth-century United States. It has been possible even in many mostly monogamous systems for a man to take a second wife if the first wife could not bear children. Such has been true for royal and aristocratic families in particular. Populations emphasizing the need for population growth, and with a relative dearth of men in particular (as in the aftermath of wars), have tended to allow the practice of polygamy, and it is a system that flourishes where wealth is measured in people, rather than in land or property.

This point about wealth in people leads to a third theme: labor and slavery. Marriage has been a way of dividing labor in the household, and wives in many cultures have done a great deal of work to support the provision of food and hospitality in particular. In such situations, polygamy enabled high-ranking men to support their larger household. In some times and places, secondary wives could be enslaved, and at points they could surmount their status as slaves by becoming plural wives and mothers. Systems of polygamy have often worked in tandem with those of slavery; both, assigning rank, were ways of exploiting labor, sometimes from the same enslaved woman who bore children and did menial tasks.

Rank and status are a fourth area of importance. Polygamy has historically been a system of inequality between men and women, but it also reveals other hierarchies, both among women and among men. Wives in such systems experienced subordination, to the husband, of course, but sometimes to other wives and women in the husband's household, including a mother-in-law or a sister-in-law. Some plural wives were managers and queens, and some were enslaved. Polygyny has tended to take place in societies that practice patrilocal marriage: that is, marriage in which wives join their husbands' communities. Such wives were often more vulnerable, far from the protection of their families. Sometimes they joined households in which a mother-in-law or a senior wife reigned supreme. In some cases, wives carried with them the rank from their families. Those who came with bridewealth, protected by complex family negotiations, tended to have greater status, while those who came in as enslaved or "chore" wives tended to have little. In general, though not always, senior or first wives had the greatest authority, though they might not be the personal favorite of the husband. Polygamy has supported masculine ambitions to authority, status, and resources. High-ranking men have practiced it most; it both augments and demonstrates their ability to command resources and people. Men speak to other men of their power by showing off their plural wives. In royal settings in particular, it has served the ambitions of the ruling dynasty, and it has been a way of incorporating tribute states, with women sent as wives to the center of power.

Since elite men predominated among those practicing polygamy, this marriage form emerged at the center of various clashes of cultures and religions, a fifth major theme. Many of the most powerful indigenous men around the world, whether among the Mixteca or the Māori, have practiced plural marriage. Two of three major monotheistic religions, Judaism and Islam, have formally allowed its practice and even occasionally encouraged it. By contrast, Christianity has mostly (though not exclusively) rejected polygamy, attempting to impose monogamy on a variety of populations. This Christian emphasis on exclusive monogamy has led to a range of conflicts, especially between Christian European missionaries and authorities and other people across the globe.

Finally, this European emphasis on monogamy, which came to be tied to Christianity and ideas about progress, has led to an association of polygamy with people, usually non-Europeans, whom Europeans deemed less civilized. Race, nation, and exclusion, then, form a sixth major theme. Ideas about polygamy, how it operates and who practices it, have contributed to racecraft and the idea that certain races have lived in particular forms of marital and sexual organization. Polygamy came to be cast as a more primitive kind of marriage, associated with indigenous people who were therefore seen as less modern. Race has thus been tied with gender and marriage regimes. Whole nations could be condemned as "backward" merely for allowing practices like polygamy to continue. Polygamy has shaped internal debates over domestic reform as well as international discussions about which nations qualify as civilized.

Polygamy, then, has marked the boundaries of progress and civilization in ways both personal and intimate and public and international. The broad history of polygamy is partly about change and the dynamic nature of debates and lived experiences of polygamy. Polygamy has altered over time and cultures. Nevertheless, its history reveals continuities, too, especially in condemnations of polygamy as an inferior marriage form. This subject illuminates with extraordinary intensity the public importance of the intimate as well as the symbolic and actual importance of marriage in defining individuals and societies. Polygamy has framed cultural contact and confrontation, the shape of empires, slavery and hierarchy, royal and aristocratic power, religion and conflict, war and expansion, race and nation. In drawing lines of civility and progress, it continues to influence the modern world in abiding ways. To understand the complicated unfolding of this process across the world, though, it helps to start a long time ago.

Chapter 1
Origins and overview

After years of childlessness, one of the most important biblical wives encouraged her husband to take another woman into his bed. In the Old Testament book of Genesis, Sarah, who was barren, suggested that her husband, Abraham, should take her maid, Hagar, as a second wife or concubine so that they could have a son. Abraham did, and Hagar bore Ishmael. Sarah then went on to bear a son, Isaac, with Abraham. The dynamics of this plural marriage became complicated, yet they also brought much-loved offspring, thus peopling the world. This situation has implied that polygamy could be, and indeed was, blessed. The tale has resonated for millennia as both a story of lived experience and an organizing mythology.

The ancient Israelite practice of polygamy echoes in other forms in various parts of the ancient and medieval world, from six continents. There were distinct iterations of polygamy in diverse political and social contexts. Overall, though, polygamy allowed for resource-building, diplomatic links, and the creation of significant networks. It was vital in numerous situations of royal power, linking the center with the regions under its control. It depended on the labor, and the endurance, of women, who were central to men's ability to mobilize people and resources. Moreover, it had implications for demographic growth, for the spacing of births by wives, and for the replacement of populations of men lost through war.

In large parts of the world in the ancient, medieval, and even modern eras, the state depended on personal power and in particular on the authority of (mostly) male rulers. In such systems, polygamy has made sense. It connected royal and aristocratic authority. It demonstrated royal masculine power, as well as augmenting it. It produced children who provided diplomatic linkages through their own relationships. It rewarded loyalty and service by high-ranking men. It established and cemented hierarchies of rank as well as gender. Linked to systems of slavery and conquest, women and their productive and reproductive labor underpinned diplomatic and political relations. For some plural wives, polygamy looked like slavery; for others, it looked like leadership.

A desire for fruitfulness in marriage propelled early practices of polygamy. The first written law code in the world, that of Hammurabi around 1780 BCE, allowed a man with a barren or diseased wife to take a second wife. At the same time, it mandated that the second wife should not be seen as equal to the first. In the biblical story in Genesis, too, polygamy stemmed from infertility. When Hagar conceived Ishmael with Abraham, "her mistress was despised in her eyes." Fertility could upend rank hierarchies, but such inversions might not last. God promised Abraham and Sarah a son, even though they were very old. After they miraculously had Isaac, Sarah became determined to send Hagar and Ishmael away; Abraham agreed to this exile. A fragile domestic equilibrium was thus re-established. God later rewarded Abraham for obedience with the covenant of enduring fruitfulness for his people: "I will multiply thy seed as the stars of the heaven, and as the sand which is upon the seashore." Between God and polygamy, Abraham was assured not just of having sons but also of having generations of descendants multiplying over the earth (Gen. 16:3–4, 22:17).

Women and children were at the center of this Genesis tale, though the Hebrew Bible overall focuses on men. This unexpected

3. This sixteenth-century engraving represents the story told in Genesis in which Abraham, at the behest of his first wife, Sarah, sent his second wife, Hagar, and their son Ishmael away.

inclusion of Sarah and Hagar, as well as young Ishmael and Isaac, highlights the centrality of women and children in a society based on kinship. The agency of women mattered a great deal, even in patriarchal societies such as ancient Israel. At the same time, the strangeness of the story and its complicated lines remind us of the considerable difficulties of knowing how polygamy has worked across times and places. While this elaborate tale in Genesis gives oblique insight into the household practices of ancient Israelites, it is shrouded in the mists of time. The practice was challenging for Sarah and Hagar, as well as Abraham, but in the end, it seems to have resolved certain problems, especially those around infertility. Given the lack of sources, though, there is much we do not know.

What we can know is that injunctions to "be fruitful and multiply" weighed most heavily on women. It was their tired and unwieldy bodies carrying pregnancies and enduring births, their breasts engorging with milk to nurse babies, their arms and backs most often carrying little ones through fields and villages. It was women who disproportionately bore the stigma and shame of childlessness and infertility. Women had an important role in the economic well-being of families. In ancient Israel, as in many other parts of the ancient and medieval world, women had an especially vital role in food processing and preparation. They did the work of grinding grain, and they baked the bread that sustained life.

Building a population depended on sex and reproduction, and in the Old Testament, plural wives often underpinned this demographic growth. Keeping those populations going required the food processing and production performed by women. The Old Testament is filled with stories of kings who gained power through the reproductive and domestic labor of multiple wives. Saul had several wives, as did David. Rehoboam had eighteen wives and sixty concubines, while Solomon had no fewer than seven hundred wives and three hundred concubines. The power of these men was counted in wives and children. Yet even Solomon received no condemnation for marrying so often; his only domestic fault was that a number of his wives came from people with whom the Israelites were not supposed to intermarry. In such systems, however, power rarely accrued to the wives themselves, despite all they did; instead it was the royal mothers of kings who claimed the greatest feminine authority. The authority of wives was too dispersed. Among the ancient Israelites, a patrilocal people, wives moved from their own communities and into those of their husbands, often ending up under the supervision of mothers-in-law and senior wives.

Senior women often had an important role in Chinese households, too, especially royal ones. In its long history, China has had a generally consistent system of formal monogamy, but with a range of concubines and "maids" allowed, even encouraged, for prosperous men. The emperor could take only one wife, but he was supposed to have multiple consorts. One second-century ruler, Sun Quan of the kingdom of Wu, was an impressive leader with a fatal flaw. He failed to distinguish between his wife and concubines; the resulting domestic chaos made him a laughingstock. Although Chinese emperors were expected to sire numerous offspring, they were not supposed to enjoy it too much; such self-indulgence was suspect in Confucian teachings. Keeping favorites, too, could be a problem. In the sixth century, the Chen emperor was supposedly so preoccupied with his favorite concubine, who sat on his lap during court business, that he lost his dynasty to attacking Sui warriors. In the sixteenth century, courtiers reminded Xianzong, the Ming emperor besotted with his favorite: "Having sons depends on there being many mothers." An empress was expected to preside over these various mothers with grace and authority. In the third century, Jin Emperor Wu received concubines from conquests, but they were vetted by the empress herself. The ancient Mao commentary praised an empress who not only avoided jealousy but also created harmony among the concubines. Wives had formally recognized children with the emperor, but so did consorts. Consorts could come from a range of backgrounds, but they and their children could rise high. In fact, the mothers of the Yongzheng, Qianlong, and Jiaqing emperors had all been bondservants.

The politics of polygamy played out differently in other settings, but here, too, there were tight connections between royal power and polygamy. In Siam, in what is now Thailand, the ruler had the authority to instigate polygamy for himself and others in the medieval and modern eras. Classic Thai Buddhist texts celebrated the potency of rulers and their plural wives, as in the *Trai Phum Phra Ruang*, a cosmology attributed to the fourteenth-century King Ruang. There was no word for polygamy in the Thai language, but the concept exists as "the principle of having many wives simultaneously." The Family Code of 1361 enshrined this principle, recognizing four legal types of wives. The first group of wives, in marriages brokered by the king himself, had the highest rank. The next category of wives were those given by their parents in protracted negotiations that preserved their inheritance and rights in the event of death or marital breakdown. The third type were those married through personal choice, lacking the family protection of the second category. The fourth and lowest-ranking wives were enslaved ones, who had little by ways of rights to inheritance or property or child custody in the event of any problems. These categories of wives mattered in terms of legal outcomes and in terms of the dynamics of these households, organizing hierarchies among the wives in these plural marriages. Enslaved wives were subject to the will and whim not only of the husband but also of other wives.

Such wifely hierarchies found their fullest expression in the Inner Palace, the household of the Thai king, where he demonstrated and augmented his power through his plural wives. Families in the provinces under the command of the ruler sent their daughters to the Inner Palace to curry favor and to ensure benevolent treatment. Such women tended to come from five categories of families. The first three categories included women from royal or politically important and office-holding families or who were related to women already there. The other two categories were wealthy families and ruling families in subordinate tribute-providing regions, seeking to prove their loyalty to the monarchy. These marriages linked the ruled to the ruler, connected the provinces to the center, and brought solidarity to the men of all of these families through their women.

Marital ties looped the state into local households in ongoing and profound ways, over decades. The children created by these unions were no less important. The sons from the Inner Palace became state officials and ensured the continuation of the monarchy. With the involvement of 176 of their wives, the first five kings of the Chakri dynasty produced 324 children, many of whom became high-ranking bureaucrats themselves.

Polygamy permeated the political culture of early modern Siam. Notable literary representations, including the Thai epic, the *Khun Chang Khun Phaen*, celebrated "having many wives simultaneously" for heroic men whose status was enhanced by such women. By contrast, the heroines were expected simply to tolerate it. For men, the important quality of *barami* (or virtue) rested on wives, without which men were considered incomplete and politically impotent. Having multiple wives and children proved the *barami* of leaders. Even in the seventeenth century, one French traveler noted, "To have a great many wives is in this country rather magnificence than debauchery. Wherefore they are very surprised to hear that so great a King as ours [Louis XIV] has no more than one wife." In one later episode, a newspaper account of Siamese court polygamy infuriated King Mongkut. He was aggrieved, not that such practices were subject to public scrutiny, but that the authors had listed more wives for his brother than for him.

Royal power showed itself in polygamy in early modern Incan, or Cuzco, society, in what is now Peru as well. Wives had vital economic and reproductive roles. One Spanish Jesuit, Bernabé Cobo, declared that "the possession of many wives was a sign of greatness and wealth among them. Only the commoners make do with one wife." In a typical European claim, Cobo went on to note that "the wives serve their husbands like slaves. They do most of the work, because besides bringing up the children, they cook, make *chicha* [a fermented ceremonial drink] and all the clothing they, their husbands, and their children wear, and they even do more work in the fields than the men." Since such assertions functioned as a way to criticize the gender and political regimes of indigenous people, it is important not to take them literally. Still, women's contributions were considerable.

These Native American plural wives had diplomatic and political significance as well. In one of the starkest connections of polygamy and political power, only the ruler of the Cuzco, the Inca himself, had the authority to confer secondary wives on a man. This royal privilege was grounded in the mythology of the empire, as origin stories conveyed that the first Inca, Maco Capac, had received secondary wives from all the nations he had invaded. In other words, polygamy could exist only where the state directly sanctioned and encouraged it, and it was often a form of tribute to the Inca.

The great power of the Inca, who controlled the distribution of wives, demonstrates the close connections between political authority and polygamy. This ability to distribute wives enhanced the power of the Inca himself, and it conferred privileges on Incan noblemen. They gave their daughters to the Inca to show their loyalty, and noblemen were rewarded with wives. Cobo noted that the Inca gave "noble and beautiful girls" to his "captains and kinsmen," concluding, "Receiving one of these virgins from the Inca personally was considered to be an extraordinary favor." Marriage intertwined with conquest because defeated peoples had to provide daughters to the Inca, for his use or to be distributed. Yet the daughters, transformed into secondary wives, kept the name of their province of origin so that the dominance of Cuzco over that region was made enduring over their lifetimes. As the rebel in one province fretted over their possible loss of sovereignty when the Inca invaded, "Foreign tyranny is at our gates.... If we yield to the Inca, we shall be obliged to give up our former freedom, our best land, our most beautiful women and girls, our customs, our laws."

Royal power in the early modern kingdom of Buganda in east Africa also increasingly intertwined with polygyny in this same era.

Here, as elsewhere, political power rested on wives. Kings linked themselves to multiple territories, including newly conquered ones, through polygamous marriages. People presented wives to the king as marks of respect or to accompany a request or to obtain forgiveness of a debt or transgression. Clans and family members established themselves by giving their women to the king's household, with a few to perform specific intimate tasks. So, the king's paternal grandmother was responsible for sending him one particular wife, the *nasaza*, responsible for cutting his hair and nails. The Otter clan had to supply another wife, the *mubugumya*, whose main duty was to warm the king's bed for him and another wife. As the kingdom expanded, wives came from raids and captivity in wars. Even high-status wives occasionally had their origins in captivity in tributary states or abduction.

This system, while enhancing masculine power, created a complicated and significant hierarchy among women. There were three main types of wives: elite wives, or ladies, who managed and organized the royal household; untitled wives; and wives from captivity or unimportant families who did much of the drudge work in the royal compounds. Wives were organized into sections, with one chief senior wife in charge of all the labor, discipline, and property distribution. These highest-ranking wives were often served themselves by their own chiefs and subchiefs who sent them tribute and taxes, thus affirming clan ties and allowing these wives to become high-ranking leaders in their own right. These plural wives were central players in state politics.

The exchange of women tied kings and their wives to lower-ranking chiefs, thus increasing centralized state power and class stratification in the early modern era. Polygyny separated well-heeled men from commoners, who could rarely afford to keep several wives. The king himself then could distribute these women as he wished to favorites, to chiefs, or to warriors. One especially colorful account of this process involved the eighteenth-century King Kamaanya, who became known for his cruelty. The king "used...to uncover his men and look at their genitals. If he saw a small man, he would scornfully comment on his size that he could never find women to love him. He would then give him about ten women to take to wife. To a huge man he would give about twenty women and again scornfully comment on his size, that he would never find enough women...to satisfy him." To be teased so intimately by a king was a mark of status and a way to secure homosocial bonds, although perhaps humiliating for individual men.

Men's relations in systems of polygamy could often have this rivalrous air. In Buganda, the king had the right to take even the wives of chiefs as his own if he so desired. Other settings similarly highlight masculine conflicts over wives and the imperial ambitions of polygamous rulers. Early seventeenth-century English observers in the land they called Virginia noted repeatedly that high-ranking local Algonkian men, especially the ambitious leader, Powhatan (or Wahunsenaca), had multiple wives. One English observer, William Strachey, was amazed at "how such a barbarous and uncivill Prince" should have "a forme and ostentacion of such Maiestie...which oftentimes strykes awe and wonder into our people." Such "ostentacion" allegedly included more than one hundred wives "according to the order and customes of sensuall Hethenisme." Another Englishman noted that this ruler lived with multiple "queens" in a house protected by one hundred armed guards.

With his marriages, Powhatan demonstrated his power in a situation of political conflict in a tense moment of imperial realignments. There had already been considerable political shifts because of long-standing enmities exacerbated by European contact and diseases. Powhatan's polygamy may have been especially "ostentatious" in order to demonstrate his authority and to forge peaceful links with tribute areas. When Powhatan received visitors, his wives flanked him, and they brought him food, water with which to wash his hands, and feathers with which to dry them. Strachey contended that a dozen women were the ruler's favorites and that they had a ranking dependent on their closeness to him. Powhatan reportedly had more than thirty children, including one of the most well-known Native American women, Pocahontas. Such children also bolstered the prestige of a ruling family; there were tight bonds between siblings. When one local leader had the audacity to abduct one of his brother's wives, Powhatan went to war and deposed him. As elsewhere, war and captivity formed a context for the abduction of women. Yet at the same time, it could support positive relations between allies. Supposedly, when Powhatan grew "weary" of certain wives, "he bestowes them on those that best deserve them." As in other contexts, the gift of wives from a ruler affirmed bonds and high rank. Others reported that Powhatan's wives from distant regions who had borne children sometimes then returned to their homelands, thus strengthening the connections between these regions and the center.

Plural marriages also established rule in more modern times among indigenous people in the Pacific Islands, including what is now Australia, New Zealand, and Papua New Guinea. One nineteenth-century missionary in New Guinea observed that "a man may have as many wives as he can afford," with headmen having up to six. This missionary lamented what he saw as the lack of harmony in polygynous families, recounting tales of conflict connected with jealousy over a favored wife. These problems threatened the whole social order: "nine-tenths of the quarrels in New Britain arise from jealousy of the women ... [and] conjugal mistrust." Imperial authors blamed indigenous polygamy and domestic rivalries for wider violence, conveniently ignoring their own settler colonialism and missionary activities. Even among European observers, though, there were accounts emphasizing domestic tranquility. Another British observer of the Māori in New Zealand was more positive, claiming that polygamy increased the power of rulers, but that all the spouses lived together in harmony. He conceded that "the *sudden* bringing home of a new wife, which sometimes happened (perhaps a slave, or from a distance)…made quite a sensation among the old wives, but it was only temporary. Often the old wives themselves encouraged their husband to take another, and aided efficiently in doing so." This statement suggests that wives could come from various backgrounds, including war, captivity, and diplomacy, a pattern found in numerous settings. It implies, too, that women had agency in the choosing of new wives and that they did not necessarily see them as a threat or simply a source of jealousy.

Harmonious and in fact helpful relations between wives have sometimes been the norm among indigenous people in the Pacific world, as more recent examples suggest. The Martu of Australia's Western Desert have long practiced polygyny, though there, as elsewhere, it is difficult to ascertain much about its roots. Marriages could be arranged, often at or shortly after birth, with family and kin networks paramount in marital decisions. Polygyny could be sororal, so that a man married multiple sisters. At least at times, wives seem to have been consulted about bringing in additional wives, and they may have instigated polygyny themselves. Some wives welcomed help with domestic work as well as the birth spacing that polygyny afforded. Older wives could help to teach younger wives, and these younger women took on menial tasks such as collecting wood and water. As one Martu woman recounted, "My sister and I were both married to the same man.…We got along very well.…Sometimes we would hunt together, or one of us would go out with our husband to get meat while the other would stay with the children and get seed or fruit." Sororal polygyny could mean that the mother of the wives lived as part of the household, thus enhancing intergenerational female links, as well as mentorship and assistance.

By contrast, European practices of polygamy, rarely involving sisters, seem to have been less friendly. Although it is often forgotten, polygamy was a long-standing practice of powerful

European kings. The ancient Roman commentator Tacitus claimed that a few Germanic kings took multiple wives not because of "lust" but because of their need for political alliances and as a way to enhance their power. The lines between wife, secondary wife, and concubine could be thin, with certain kinds of unions receiving more formal recognition. The sagas of Old Norse kings suggest that the practices of polygamy and concubinage were connected here, as elsewhere, with systems of slavery. Scholars have debated how polygamous the Merovingian kings were, but most agree that they were anything but monogamous, keeping wives and concubines as it seemed best for policy or personal ambitions. In a few instances, such rulers had children with enslaved concubines and subsequently freed and married them, so there are accounts of Merovingian queens of humble origins, much to the dismay of hierarchical, monogamy-focused commentators such as Gregory of Tours.

Medieval Irish kings, too, could have plural wives. By the eighth century, there were debates in legal texts about whether it was acceptable for Irish Christians to "live in plurality of unions," with citations of the Old Testament polygamy of Solomon, David, and Jacob. These references imply long-standing Irish traditions of polygamy. There was clear endorsement in certain circles of a man taking a second wife if his first could not have children; moreover, there seems to have been political polygamy to knit together various kingdoms and communities. Other legal texts distinguished between two major types of wives: a primary wife, who ran the household, and a "betrothed" or secondary wife, who was her subordinate. One such tract distinguished further: between a primary wife with sons (the highest status), a primary wife without sons, a betrothed (or secondary) wife, the "acknowledged woman" not betrothed (a concubine), and, finally, a "woman who has been abducted."

This reference to abduction of women as a route to marriage, a custom that continued for centuries, reminds us of the violence that could underpin domestic regimes in early medieval Ireland. Relations between these wives, too, were not necessarily peaceful. Legal codes acknowledged the "lawful jealousy" of the primary wife and its sometimes brutal consequences. Indeed, the law enshrined the right of the primary wife to be "completely free from liability for anything she may do during the first three nights" after the arrival of the secondary wife—short of killing her. For her part, the secondary wife had "the right to inflict damage with her finger-nails and to utter insults and scratchings and hair-tearings and small injuries in general." Polygamy could be a brawl between women, at least according to these legal texts.

In Ireland, polygamy could be fraught among offspring as well as wives. While the son of the primary wife was preferred for succession, he could be bested by the son of the secondary wife if the latter seemed better qualified to rule. The twelfth-century king of Connacht, Ruaidrí Ua Conchobair, had several wives and children. The pope supposedly offered to let him keep his six wives and still be recognized as the king of Ireland if he would agree to renounce any further wives. However, he would not accept these terms, and so, as the annals conclude, "God took the rule and sovranty from his seed for ever, in punishment for his sin." Even a few European kings were loath to give up polygamy.

Yet, as this story of the Irish king suggests, the practice of polygamy never won the approval of the Catholic Church, no matter how powerful a few of its practitioners were. Numerous societies allowed both polygamy and monogamy as forms of union; usually, the former was the practice of the wealthy and powerful. Increasingly, the systems allowing both kinds of unions would come into contact with those in which monogamy was considered the only acceptable option. To understand the complexities of these encounters, it is useful to turn to the history of polygamy in the three great monotheistic religions: Christianity, Judaism, and Islam.

Chapter 2
Monotheism

In the sixteenth-century Ottoman Empire, the deviant passions of the sultan provoked a scandal. In his harem in the Old Palace, women whispered in disbelief about what he was doing; no one could recall behavior like his. When news of his questionable choices emerged widely, viziers and pashas tutted over the political implications of the sultan's sex life. "He has so astonished all his subjects that they say [he is] bewitched," declared a visiting Venetian, Luigi Bassano. How else to explain a break with precedent so dangerous it could imperil the entire empire?

This sultan, Suleyman, had shocked the world by becoming... monogamous. Circumventing the usual system of concubinage, he had fallen hard for an enslaved, formerly Christian woman, Roxelana. This was not supposed to happen. As Bassano observed, "'The Grand Turk has a palace of women.... There he keeps a great number of young Christian slave girls.... From these the Grand Turk chooses whoever pleases him the most." To please the emperor was to become *gözde*, "in the eye of the sultan," someone of significance in the palace hierarchy. To bear him a child, especially a son, was to gain political status. Such a mother ceased to be a slave and instead became a potential queen mother and thus very important. Yet, usually, this moment of the concubine becoming the mother of a son was the point at which the sultan then ended sexual contact with her. She was transformed from a lover to a mother, and the latter mattered more. But Suleyman refused to give up Roxelana even after she bore him sons.

Monogamy could be as outrageous as polygamy in certain contexts. Although Westerners have long imagined the Ottoman harem as a space of libertinism, in fact, it could be like a women's college or even a convent: a highly ordered, hierarchical institution of learning and religion for females (all the non-Muslim enslaved women were taught Islam, literacy, and ladylike pursuits such as embroidery). The harem offered enslaved foreign women, and their supporters in the palace, a chance to become powerful and wealthy. Suleyman, new to the throne, freed Roxelana and then married her; they had six children. Even more stunning, he then moved her and their children into the formerly all-male New Palace. This unexpected marital monogamy by an Ottoman emperor gummed up the works of a long-established system. Usually, sons of different concubines competed to become sultan, supported by particular backers in the court. Suleyman and Roxelana shifted inheritance to ensure that only Roxelana's sons could become sultan, thus cutting off Suleyman's other sons from any chance of succession. They thus altered a tradition of Ottoman leadership that depended on the political links established by concubines and the sons sent to serve in outlying regions. So, this novel system gave one wife, Roxelana, and her sons unprecedented power, disturbing others in the court. Monogamy could be a powerful choice among Muslims, as well as among Jews and Christians.

Despite shared Abrahamic faith in a single God, Judaism, Islam, and Christianity in fact diverged in terms of polygamy. Judaism and Islam agreed on its basic legality while recognizing its challenges. Christianity, especially Catholicism, stood out for its insistent emphasis on monogamy and rejection of polygamy up to the era of the Protestant Reformation and beyond. Yet, at the same time, there was never total unity in any of these major faiths, and polygamy provoked debates, at levels high and low, among ordinary women and men and among the learned elite. Some Muslims, including Suleyman and Roxelana, endorsed monogamy, in their case despite the scandal it occasioned. For their part, at least a few notable Christians suggested that there might be circumstances when polygamy was acceptable. Jews, too, divided on this issue. The sacred books of all three faiths contained clear and compelling examples of holy men—and women—who lived in polygamy: a vexing inheritance for Christians in particular. Abraham (or Ibrahim) is a holy prophet in all three religions, and his choice to take Hagar as a secondary wife or concubine resonated in all three religious traditions.

Although there was a basic divergence between two major streams, Christianity on the one hand and Judaism and Islam on the other, the waters that ran between them were not crystal clear. Indeed, at certain points and in particular contexts, they could be quite muddy. Moreover, adherents of these faiths often rubbed along together, especially in places like the Middle East and Iberia, where Muslim, Jews, and Christians had lived in the same areas for centuries. They thus influenced each other, sometimes encouraging polygamy (as for Jews living amid Muslims in medieval Spain), sometimes discouraging it (as for Jews living amid Christians in increasingly intolerant times in central and eastern Europe in this same era).

The injunction "to be fruitful and multiply" in Genesis has towered over all of these religions, including Judaism. The story of Abraham, Sarah, and Hagar, as well as the examples of other wise and holy leaders such as David and Solomon, suggested that polygyny could be a sanctioned practice. Injunctions in Deuteronomy 25 underpinned Jewish polygyny: "If brethren dwell together, and one of them die, and have no child ... her husband's brother shall go in unto her, and take her to him to wife." This practice of what is termed levirate marriage meant that a man whose brother died had the responsibility, sometimes enforced, sometimes not, of marrying his sister-in-law even if he was already married himself. In fact, the Mishnah, the first work of written Jewish law stemming from oral traditions, declared that even if four brothers all died at the same time, the surviving brother could and should marry all four widows at once.

The practice of polygyny was acceptable, if not necessarily frequent, among Jewish communities of all sorts in the period after the destruction of the Second Temple in 70 CE continuing into the medieval period. In the first century CE, the Jewish historian Josephus observed that having several wives at the same time was an ancient custom, but most Jews in this period seem to have been monogamous. The Mishnah refers to polygamy as an accepted but not necessarily common tradition, working out some of the details of how it should operate among communities of the faithful. For example, it stated that a man should take more than one wife only if he could support all his wives and children. The Babylonian Talmud from the fifth century echoes such teachings.

Yet there seems to have been a growing preference for monogamy. It may be that women and their families were agents in this change. Although the Talmud and other authoritative texts do not always explain how the presence of wives and their families shaped Jewish custom, other sources provide insights. In the period from the ninth century on, in keeping with rabbinic teachings, Jews in Cairo did not throw away texts that had any holy words on them but instead deposited them in a *genizah*, a kind of holy storage area. They included a range of legal rulings and contracts, excavated in the late nineteenth century. This extraordinary cache of documents, especially rich for the periods from the ninth to thirteenth centuries, reveals both the practice of Jewish polygamy in Cairo and the curbs put on it, partly driven by first wives and their families demanding monogamy in marriage contracts. Polygamy in Cairo was largely, but not exclusively, an elite practice, and some of the most important leaders in this community had more than one wife.

Yet medieval Egyptian Jewish women, backed by their families, included stipulations in their marriage contracts that the husband could not take a second wife. The number of monogamy clauses seems to have increased in the late eleventh and early twelfth centuries. In one twelfth-century contract, one man agreed that he would take a second wife only with his first wife's consent. He further stated that if she agreed and the arrangement subsequently proved untenable to her, he would give her a divorce, repaying her full marriage settlement. The contract noted the presence of one formidable witness: "Her mother is present and hears all this." Other contracts stipulated that a husband would be fined if he took a second wife, or an enslaved concubine, of whom the wife disapproved. In another contract, the parties agreed to several points, all of which pointed to the agency of the bride and her family. The groom promised that he would join his wife and live with his in-laws in their house, and the couple would not move or travel without the wife's consent. He noted that he would have no claim to her earnings during the marriage. Finally, he acknowledged that if he took an enslaved woman as a concubine without her approval, or took a second wife at all, she had the right to divorce and the return of her full marriage settlement.

These clauses from marriage contracts in the Cairo *genizah* suggest that medieval Jewish wives (and/or their kin) preferred monogamy and husbands often conceded to this preference, at least legally. Further, they imply that wives and their families would have rather had a husband take an enslaved concubine than a second wife. Families negotiating these settlements seem to have been less threatened by an enslaved woman who had no competing claims than by a second wife who did. It may be that wives themselves felt less insecure about a woman who was enslaved and thus at their service, or it might reflect concerns of their natal families. In one eleventh-century prenuptial contract, the husband-to-be agreed to give up his drinking companions and dissolute behavior, promising he would buy an enslaved woman only with the explicit permission of his wife. This clause suggests that all parties presumed he would want to do so and that the wife might agree to it.

Other Jewish communities were even more favorably disposed to polygamy, such as Karaite Jews living in Muslim lands around this same period. They took the injunction "to be fruitful and multiply" to mean that if a wife had not had a child in ten years of marriage, the husband *had* to take a second wife. Still, even then, the husband had to provide the first wife with her own separate home so that she did not have to witness the intimacies between the husband and the second wife. The Jerusalem Talmud, dating from the fourth century, included a tale about thirteen married brothers. All but one died childless. Their rabbi, offering to help pay maintenance costs, enjoined the surviving brother to perform his levirate duty by marrying all twelve widows. Some years on, this brother with his thirteen wives had no fewer than thirty-six children: a triumph of fruitfulness witnessed with joy by the rabbi and the larger community. The noted twelfth-century Spanish scholar Moses ben Maimon, better known as Maimonides, discussed the practice of polygyny repeatedly, concluding that "a man may marry several wives, even one hundred... and his wife may not prevent him, provided he can supply each one with the food, clothing, and conjugal rights that are due to her. But he may not compel them to dwell in one courtyard, but rather each one by herself." Such a statement put the husband's preferences well before the wife's, but even here, acknowledged that each wife had the right to her own dwelling space.

These diverse customs demonstrate the variety among Jewish communities in the diaspora. Indeed, practices of Jewish polygamy would ultimately take one of two major routes. The Sephardim, scattered in the Middle East and Iberia among Muslims, continued to allow and occasionally to practice polygyny, though usually of a limited sort, mostly involving the wealthy and/or levirate marriages. Ashkenazi communities in eastern Europe, surrounded by Christians, came to reject the practice under a thousand-year ban, or *herem*, attributed to Rabbi Gershom ben Judah around 1030 CE, likely instituted at a council of scholars at Worms. (It was renewed in 2000.) In 1030, it may have been confirming what was already typical practice among Jews in these areas and/or demonstrating Jewish alignment with Christian marriage principles. In just this era, the Crusades were making divergence from Christian customs a more dangerous enterprise for Jews living amid Christians. This ban on polygyny among the Ashkenazim may have been part of long-standing internal reforms that supported the rights of first wives. Whatever the root cause, this curtailment became widely accepted; by the early twelfth century, Rabbi Eliezer ben Nathan noted that while polygyny was "the rule in former generations...in our generation, one cannot marry a second wife" even when the first wife was ill or infertile. Although the Sephardim continued to accept limited polygyny, among the Ashkenazim, monogamy trumped even the ideal of fertility or the demands of levirate marriage.

Monogamy also trumped fruitfulness—and the practice of polygamy by Old Testament patriarchs—for both Roman Catholics and Eastern Orthodox Christians. The Christian preference for monogamy stemmed more from Greco-Roman customs than from the words of Jesus or the apostles, reflecting that Roman law emphasized a single wife. Ancient Romans enshrined formal legal monogamy, while permitting an unmarried man to take concubines. Legal marriage, a private contract, was allowed only between citizens, and it was a form of alliance between high-ranking families. Slaves were not permitted to marry, though they could be taken as additional partners by a citizen with a legal wife. Ancient Romans emphasized legal monogamous marriage to protect the status of Roman citizens and to ensure clear lines of inheritance. Only sons of the legal wife could inherit from their father. The Roman jurist Gaius noted c. 170 CE that a "woman cannot marry two men, nor can a man have two wives." Third-century laws, recorded in the code of Justinian, declared that "it is allowed to no one who is under Roman authority to be able to have two wives openly," with "infamy" attending men who tried to do so. When the Roman Empire became a Christian one, the emphasis on monogamy only increased. In 393, Emperor Theodosius explicitly prohibited polygamy and other "Jewish" marriage customs.

Again, monogamy marked out and distinguished Christians, with their Greco-Roman legal systems, from other peoples. Early church fathers, in both the Eastern and the Western traditions, rejected polygamy for Christians. They may have been inspired by the emphasis on Adam and Eve, the monogamous couple par excellence, as well as by the idea that Christ took the church as his single bride. In other words, monogamy was a powerful symbol, especially as Christians established their monotheistic credentials. Yet those holy polygamous patriarchs in the Old Testament vexed them, especially since nothing and no one in the New Testament explicitly condemned polygamy. In the fourth century, John Chrysostom, archbishop of Constantinople, conceded that in Old Testament times "people were allowed to have two or more wives as to increase the race," but this imperative no longer carried weight. That same century, Augustine of Hippo agreed that before Jesus's time, it was customary for a man to have several wives, especially for the purposes of reproduction. The fact that husbands had their wife's permission to take a second wife, or had even been encouraged to do by their first wife, as in the case of Sarah, Abraham, and Hagar, showed how acceptable it had been in times past. However, such need for population growth was no longer an imperative for Christians. Still, Augustine, emphasizing marriage as a way lawfully to have children, conceded that polygamy purely for procreation was preferable to a monogamy driven by lust: "I approve the man who exploits the fertility of many women for a purpose other than sex more highly that one who enjoys one woman's flesh for its own sake."

The Crusades energized these ideals of Christian monogamy, as theologians worried over the population growth of Muslims in particular with ever more lurid condemnations. In the thirteenth century, Matthew Paris fretted, "Mohamet instituted polygamy... only so that by propagating he could increase his race and people, and thus strengthen his law by number." At the start of the thirteenth century, Pope Innocent III declaimed that polygamy was illegal because Jesus has described marriage as "two in one flesh," not as "three or four." Such prohibitions appear as well in the standard work of thirteenth-century canon law, the *Decretals*. In a slightly later era, Jacques de Vitry's *Historia Orientalis* (1596) explicitly denounced Muslim practices of polygyny and the "lusts" of those who lived in warmer regions. He worried that Muslims, or Saracens, as he termed them, "ensnared by carnal lures" could therefore be "multiplied beyond number," overtaking Christian populations.

These Christian writers agreed that polygamy violated Christian law and the teachings of Jesus and the church. Yet opinion remained divided about whether it broke natural law as well. Several notable theologians, including Augustine, contended that polygamy might be compatible with natural law, especially in times of war or other catastrophes. John Duns Scotus in the thirteenth century, Durandus of Saint Pourçain in the fourteenth, and Tommaso de Vio, Cardinal Cajetan, in the early sixteenth century, all concurred that while "plurality of wives" was against Christian law, it was not against natural law. Gerard Odonis, a fourteenth-century French Franciscan, noted that polygamy, unlike adultery and divorce, was only prohibited by canon law, not by the Bible, so polygamy might be a better option than adultery or divorce in cases of a need for a royal heir.

As in Christianity and Judaism, ancient polygamy influenced marriage law and customs among Muslims. "Hagar was a female slave of special mien," announced a ninth-century account of Ibrahim (or Abraham), Sarah, and Hagar. This tale, related by the scholar al-Tabari based on an earlier version by one of Muhammad's earliest biographers, Ibn Ishaq, continued: "Sarah gave her to Abraham, saying: 'I view her as a pure woman, so take her. Perhaps God will bestow a son upon you from her,' for Sarah had grown old without bearing children....Thereupon, Abraham had relations with Hagar, and she bore him Ishmael." Ibrahim, or Abraham, was a holy progenitor for Muslims, as for Jews and Christians. The Qu'ran calls him "a leader for the people" (surah 2:12) and celebrates him as an ancestor who believed in God and monotheism. There is even a chapter of the Qu'ran denoted "Ibrahim" (surah 14).

The basic plotline of Ibrahim, Sarah, and Hagar in Islamic traditions follows similar lines to that in the Old Testament, but later versions elaborated on it in slightly different ways. In some tellings, Hagar was elevated to a relation of a king, not simply an enslaved woman, and Ishmael often had a more important role. In others, there was attention to the complicated relations between the two wives. One eleventh-century account by a Persian scholar recounted that Sarah was furious when Ibrahim, following the rule of primogeniture, promised his inheritance to Ishmael rather than Isaac, even though Hagar was merely an enslaved and secondary wife. As the story puts it, "female jealousy had taken ahold of her. She swore to cut off a piece of [Hagar's] flesh." Abraham convinced Sarah merely to bore a hole in Hagar's ear, so that "it became a custom among women" to pierce their ears. Some of these traditions suggested that Abraham brought Hagar and Ishmael to Mecca, where Ishmael and Abraham, following God's commands, built the Ka'ba, the sacred center of Islamic pilgrimage there.

Muhammad, the Prophet of Islam, set a precedent for Muslims by marrying more than one woman, though he was likely following local custom. In fact, he was monogamous for decades, married to Khadijah, who bore most of his children. He married again only when she had passed away, and it was at this point that he took several wives, likely to protect vulnerable women or to establish political connections. It is not clear whether all these marriages, which included women young and old, were consummated. The

Qu'ran termed such wives "mothers of the faithful," establishing them as paragons of female virtue. The Qu'ran advised men that four wives was the limit: "marry such women as seem good to you, two, three, four; but if you fear you will not be equitable, then only one" (surah 4:2).

When one of Muhammad's companions converted to Islam, the Prophet advised him to choose four wives, "releasing" the others, which he did. This advice suggests some accommodation and amelioration of local practices, rather than a positive injunction against polygyny. It has meant that polygyny among Muslims is technically limited to four wives. Its practice further requires that the husband follow principles of justice and fairness between the wives, ensuring that they are treated and supported equitably. Older Islamic laws, like ancient Roman ones, permitted a man to engage in sexual relations with unmarried enslaved women.

Islamic communities have differed over time and place in how they have lived out these teachings on polygyny. Islamic law, the *shari'a*, is a fluid and flexible system, and it can be interpreted in different ways. In addition to the well-known distinctions between Shi'ite and Sunni, there are four major schools of Sunni legal thought. Legal scholars shape interpretations, as do states and regimes, as well as ordinary people. Early Islamic law generally supported the idea that men were providers and women were dependents. By allowing polygyny and concubinage, the law broadly fixed the idea that men could have multiple legal sexual partners while women could not. Still, within this general understanding, there has been room for considerable female agency. For instance, early Islamic law allowed a woman, whether unmarried or married, full possession of her own property, a marked contrast with more constricted Europeans laws of the era.

Under Islamic law, plural wives have had rights to equal time as well as the financial resources and the "pleasure and companionship'" of the husband. There were debates, though, over how this might work in practice; for instance, should a man spend one night or longer with each wife? Moreover, there were some exceptions. When a man married a new woman, he could spend additional time with her: an entire week for a virgin bride and three nights with a wife who had been married previously. If one wife did not want his company on her allotted night, he was free to go to another one. A husband had the right to take only one wife with him on a journey, but there was disagreement among experts as to whether he was allowed to choose freely or whether he had to draw lots. There was further controversy over whether non-Muslim or enslaved wives should have the same rights as free Muslim wives.

Despite these rules surrounding polygyny, the dominant practice of Islamic marriage in most areas was monogamy. Not many men could support the larger households and large number of children of polygyny, and it created a more complicated family structure. The first Abbasid caliphs in the eighth century allowed for inclusion of antipolygamy clauses in marriage agreements, reflecting that there was resistance to it from wives and their families. At the same time, though, they instituted concubinage of enslaved women as a means of royal reproduction, a practice later taken up by the Ottomans. This practice was limited to rulers. In Egyptian provincial towns in the eighth and ninth centuries, for Muslims as for Jews, some brides and their families included contractual stipulations that the husband could not take a second wife without their consent. Again, local practices may have partly dictated these customs. Part of the reason that Ottoman sultans took non-Muslim women as enslaved lovers, then transforming them into concubines and mothers, was that such a practice avoided the need to undertake complicated marital negotiations with imperial families. So, in systems of polygamy and concubinage, there is a complicated intersection of slavery and sex. Differentials of status between wives mattered a great deal, too. First and senior wives helped to shape marriage practices, yet so did even enslaved women, taken as concubines or secondary wives in systems of considerable status disparities.

In some Muslim communities, such as those in fifteenth-century Cairo, the practice of polygamy was legal but extremely limited. Women themselves seem largely to have preferred monogamy, and their desires came to dominate. When the sultan of Cairo agreed to hear petitions from common folk in 1471, in an experiment with more hands-on royal rule typical of such leaders, one woman came forward to complain that her husband had taken a second wife. The sultan was not especially pleased to hear from a lowly woman about marital unhappiness; indeed, it caused him to curtail the entire experiment in direct royal justice. Nevertheless, the fact that an ordinary woman assumed that even the sultan would be on her side in her rejection of polygamy indicates how widely accepted this stance was among the people in her community. In another exceptional source, a collection of more than a thousand biographies of notable women in fifteenth-century Egypt and Syria, there were a few stories of monogamous wives who instigated divorces, thus suggesting the larger agency of wives in households. At least one case for divorce was related to a rejection of polygamy. However, the relative silence around polygamy in these records suggests that it was unusual even in prosperous households in this period.

Wives and their families had concerns about the dispersal of economic resources among multiple wives, as well as possible jealousy. As in Jewish communities in Egypt, enslaved female concubines provoked less worry than secondary wives, but most first wives preferred that their husbands have neither. Husbands often, though not always, acceded to these wishes. In one notable biography of a Muslim scholar from fifteenth-century Egypt, the scholar, Ibn Hajar, had a wife, Uns, who bore only daughters. He wanted to take a second wife, but he did not do so, out of deference to Uns's wishes. He had the right to sex with their enslaved women, but he knew that such activity would be unacceptable to his wife. He ended up secretly transferring ownership of an enslaved woman, Hass Turk, from his wife to himself so that he could keep this concubine, and the son she then bore, secret. When his wife found out, he agreed to end the relationship. Although the biography marginalized Hass Turk's agency, she had an important role. She could have told the wife sooner, so that she was not sold away. Her complicity allowed the relationship to establish itself. Moreover, once she had a child, she and the child both had rights. She was guaranteed freedom at her master's death and her son had the right to freedom and paternal inheritance. This is far from the harem of orientalist cliché, and the wishes of both of the women involved made a difference in how this situation played out.

The wishes of wives likely shaped the relatively limited role polygamy played in later eras of the Ottoman Empire, such as in the eighteenth and nineteenth centuries. In Ottoman Syria and Palestine, polygyny was permitted, but rare. The *muftis*, or religious leaders, did not discuss it much, thus suggesting it was infrequent and not the subject of much controversy. Polygyny, like concubinage, was expensive, since both required financial support for the women and their children. Therefore, it was limited, mostly to the rich. There were a few instances of plural marriages further down the social scale, but serial monogamy with divorce was more common among this population. In the Palestinian town of Nablus, from 1720 to 1858, estate lists for sixty-two men reveal that ten had two wives and one had three. So, while plural marriages were certainly in the minority, they existed as a known practice. Here, as elsewhere, though, monogamy often prevailed, even where polygamy existed.

Still, overall, despite common emphasis on Abraham, Sarah, and Hagar as holy ancestors, Judaism, Christianity, and Islam took divergent routes in terms of polygamy. Muslims and, to a lesser extent, Jews have accepted its practice, at least in theory, and they have mandated how it might work, trying to ensure legal protection for wives and their children. While it is rarely the practice of the majority and is often quite limited, it still has existed as a possibility for the faithful. Christians, following the laws and customs of polytheistic Romans, largely rejected the practice. These distinct paths created conflict when these cultures came into contact in new ways in the early modern era.

Chapter 3
Early modern encounters

"Father, if a king like me wishes to become Christian and has many wives, what would you do with him?" enquired the Mughal Muslim emperor, Jahangir, to a Jesuit in the early seventeenth century. The missionary responded that a Christian king would have to choose one single wife and leave the others. "This," replied Jahangir in exasperation, "would be very difficult." Such a dialogue resonated throughout the era, as global contacts reshaped empires. As European Christians, committed to monogamy as an organizing principle, moved into that world, they found many people living in plural marriages. To these people, Christian insistence on monogamy was strange and unwelcome. Forcing a transition from polygamy to monogamy on high-ranking men certainly caused "difficulties." Polygamy was a system supporting the authority of rulers around the world, so it was often at the center of disputes between such leaders and European missionaries and colonizers.

A global clash between monogamy and polygamy was a key aspect of the early modern era, one that pitted Christians against Muslims, Jews, pagans, and "apostates" of all descriptions. The correct practice of marriage was integral to imperial projects all over the globe even as marital practices changed as a result of realignments and resettlements. As Europeans moved into the wider world in greater numbers, they came upon emperors who not only practiced polygamy but also were increasingly doing so for political reasons, to increase wealth and to link outlying regions through marital connections. European missionaries viewed polygamy only as an obstacle, an indicator of heathenism, the mark of infidels. Catholic missionaries were keenest to convert powerful men, exactly those most likely to be practicing polygamy. In a busy world of men seeking to prove their prowess to other men, as well as in building states and empires, marital status, and polygamy, shaped these encounters. In three expansionist polygamous cultures, those of the Aztecs in what is now Mexico, the Mughals in what is now India and Pakistan, and the kingdom of Dahomey in what is now Benin, polygamy continued because of its vital significance to political structures.

Polygamy became politically important in what is now called the Aztec Empire, in city states such as Tenochtitlan and Texcoco. The indigenous people called themselves Nahuas. Origin stories recounted by indigenous chroniclers showcased the importance of imperial practices of polygamy. When Acamapichtli, the leader of the ruling city, Tenochtitlan, found that his wife was barren, outlying tribute states gave him wives: "All the ancient Mexica...each gave a daughter to their ruler so that he would have children, his seed would spread and thus there would be noblemen and rulers." Each wife had children who then controlled each tribute state. This origins story, whether true or not, showed that the power of the empire emanated to each distant location by marriage and the peaceful links connecting them to the ruler: symbolic both of the diplomatic and fruitful interconnections and of the superiority and control of the central powers at Tenochtitlan. When the Spanish arrived in Mexico in 1519, they noted that noble men, especially the rulers or *tlahtoani*, had multiple wives. Since polygyny required a large and therefore expensive household, it was generally the practice of the wealthy.

Aztec plural wives obtained household rank through their seniority and status. There was a primary wife, usually the first, who had the highest status. Her sons would inherit rank and property. Noblemen sought to elevate their status through marriages to high-ranking women, to marry up, as it were, so that the offspring of the union would be able to call on the support of powerful relations. One indigenous chronicler noted that the ruler of Tollan had become its head because "his mother was from there," married to another ruler. These maternal connections were significant to the son's political rise. In addition, there were secondary wives and concubines, some of whom could be lower-ranking or even captive women. One great fifteenth-century ruler, Itzcóatl, was the son of the first Mexica ruler, Acamapichtli, and a woman who sold vegetables at the market and had likely been enslaved. He was not supposed to be the heir, but he seized his opportunities to become the leader. The system allowed for a variety of types of wives, along with a certain amount of jockeying for inheritance and rule. While such competitions benefitted ambitious men like Acamapichtli, they could also lead to wars between regions, as states defended the inheritances of the offspring of the wife from that region. In more peaceful times, women could be given as secondary wives to strengthen connections between states.

The labor that Aztec wives and concubines did was critical to the status of the larger household. They bore children and thus strengthened networks of family, and they provided hospitality. They produced cloth: a highly marketable commodity, a tribute item, and a marker of prestige. Women of all ranks spun thread, wove cloth, and embroidered it. As one Franciscan noted in 1540, wealthy men enjoyed benefits from this cloth production by their numerous wives. This same friar contended that some men "had two hundred wives . . . [as] a means of profit, because they set all the women weaving cloth."

To become a respected secondary wife or concubine, working in specialized cloth design and production with occasional visits from the master, was likely a role that lower-ranking women might have found appealing or at least preferable to the alternative. For them, monogamy, with its mucky and relentless labor of a less specialized sort and the need to care for children on their own, may have been less attractive. Such systems therefore supported the ambitions of ordinary women, who found a way to advance themselves and their children socially and economically through polygamy. In addition, they bolstered the prestige and resources of the household of the master and the other wives and concubines. As one friar reported in 1529, polygamy was a major social issue, as noblemen could have up to four hundred wives while other "men live miserably cheated."

In the fourteenth century, there was a considerable imperial expansion, as rulers of city states like Tenochtitlan enlarged their territory. They conquered weaker neighbors, turning them into tribute states. This territorial growth worked together with an increase in polygamy. These leaders demanded and married daughters of rulers of tribute states, thus establishing enduring links with the outlying territories. The daughters of the emperor married leaders of tribute states, so that state power depended on this network of linked and allied households. Wives of the ruler represented states, so that favoring one wife over another was a potent political statement. The Codex Chimalpahin, a historical account by an indigenous author, enumerated the marriages of the daughters of Moctezuma (Motecuhzoma or Montezuma) II throughout the empire; their husbands included "a Spanish conquistador" as well as members of the indigenous elite. Leaders distributed such women to their loyal nobility through polygamous marriages. Building what became the triple alliance of Tenochtitlan, Texcoco, and Tlacopan went hand in hand with an expansion of polygamy. Both empire and polygamy increased further under Moctezuma Ilhuicamina (who died in 1468) and his fellow ruler, Nezahualpilli of Texcoco (r. 1471–1515), who reportedly had more than two thousand wives and concubines. By the time the Spanish arrived to meet Moctezuma II, they found that he had hundreds of wives across several palaces. Yet such extensive polygyny may have been a relatively recently established tradition among these rulers, showing control of an array of regions and states.

Needless to say, the Spanish, and particularly the Franciscans, worked hard to end this practice among the indigenous populations. They persuaded the Spanish queen to issue a *cédula*, or royal order, requiring that a converted Indian choose one single legitimate wife recognized by the church and the state, thus basically abandoning the remaining wives and children. Franciscans publicly humiliated and flogged some men who flouted this rule. One Franciscan, Fray Toríbio de Benavente, or Motolinía, condemned polygyny as "an ancient carnal custom that greatly embraced sensuality." To his dismay, he found that "neither entreaties, threats, sermons nor anything else sufficed to make them give up all these wives." At church synods in 1533, 1537, and 1539, members agreed that these domestic and sexual practices were obstacles to conversion. There were some victories for the missionaries: leaders adopted monogamy in Tepoztlan, Tepetenchic, and Panchimalco. The ruler of Acxotlan apparently agreed to give up four of his five wives after a visit from a friar.

Yet polygamy was an important political, economic, and social institution among people who saw marriage as a civil, not religious, act that could be ended through divorce or practiced as a single or plural union. It was especially valuable for high-ranking men. Missionaries worked hard to instill the notion that marriage should be monogamous, sacramental, and lifelong, but this transition was not so easily achieved. Franciscans complained that Christian baptized *tlahtoani* (leaders) still had what the friars called, disparagingly, "concubines." In the region of Morelos in the late 1530s, one such leader had one wife and six concubines. A second had five wives, of whom four were baptized. A third had no fewer than seventeen. Yet all admitted their polygyny to authorities, apparently seeing no incompatibility between their multiple spouses and their Christianity.

Monogamy did eventually win ascendancy, but this transition may have had as much to do with internal dynamics as with the zeal of Franciscan monks. Spanish law, which became dominant, recognized only monogamous lines of inheritance, so that polygamy no longer offered as much advantage for women and their children. The crumbling of traditional tribute systems, in which polygamy augmented political and economic capital, meant that it was no longer as attractive. Women, seeing these changes in policies, began to insist on monogamy to protect the futures of their children in the new colonial order, where illegitimacy could be a barrier to advancement. Wealthy primary wives may have decided that there was too much to be lost from their husband taking a secondary wife or concubine.

Such conflicts over the continued practice of polygamy in the colonial era could become extremely heated. One notable sixteenth-century situation in Texcoco involved a baptized indigenous leader, Don Carlos, the son of a ruler and a concubine. Don Carlos had an arranged marriage. Nevertheless, he seems to have pursued his interest in other women, which put him firmly in the crosshairs of the Mexican Inquisition. It did not end well for him, because he was taken to trial, excommunicated, and burned to death. The trial documents afford extraordinary glimpses into these fights over marriage and status among indigenous people. Don Carlos apparently berated his own sister, Doña Maria, who had complained about his treatment of his wife. Don Carlos asserted his prerogative against the sniping of both Spanish Franciscans and the women in his family. He started with his sister's own marriage, reminding her of her traditional wifely duties to accept other wives: "You have to do whatever your husband wants and needs. I think that you do not follow what our ancestors used to do. If your husband wants to take other women, you do not impede him or scold the women that he takes or pay attention to the matrimonial laws of the Christians." This admonition suggests that she may well have been directing anger at her husband and

44

the lover(s) he had taken, asserting her own desires with the backing of Christian teachings. Don Carlos continued: "I am also married, but... I do not refrain from taking your niece as my concubine. If I want to lay with her and if my wife is angry, so what, it is nothing." This last statement implies that his sister was backing his wife and that both women were angry with the exploitation of this younger female relative. In this story of polygamy, there seem to have been points of conflict between women over rank and sex, yet moments of solidarity, of wives banding together, as well. In situations in which polygamy ended, it often had as much or more to do with indigenous preferences, changing economics, and new legal and political realities as with the attempts at its abolition by Franciscans and other European Christians.

The Mughal Empire, too, reveals the complicated dynamics of polygamy and imperial expansion. Mughal growth in the sixteenth and seventeenth centuries involved the transformation of the imperial harem. The marriages of Jahangir, the fourth Mughal emperor from 1605, underpinned his rule. He was by then a mature man, with several wives, concubines, and children. Exactly how many he had was not clear even to contemporary observers. English sojourners estimated anywhere from four to a thousand; Portuguese Jesuits reckoned five hundred, both vast overestimates typical of European travelers. Jahangir himself recorded nineteen. These same European writers contended that the emperor chose wives based on their beauty, but in fact it was largely a political choice. Jahangir married the daughters of rajas and other rulers from tribute states. The harem was here, as elsewhere, a location of political significance.

As in the Ottoman Empire, the Mughal harem offered women, especially more senior ones, opportunities, what one scholar has termed "wide horizons behind high walls." Older women there advised the emperor, protected and guided princes, and instructed younger women and wives. The harem was a place of learning and study, where women wrote poetry and debated politics. Favorite wives often took on a leading role in the harem. One imperial wife, Nur Jahan, in fact became a cosovereign with her husband, Jahangir. Her rise depended not only on her formidable intelligence, courage, and skill, but also on her impressive parents and the guidance of older women in the harem. She was the first Mughal woman to issue orders and to mint coins in her own name. Issuing edicts and coins were two major markers of sovereignty and quite exceptional. She was celebrated at the time as a skilled hunter, in one notable encounter killing four tigers with a mere six shots from the back of a moving elephant. She and Jahangir seem to have been devoted to each other, and art of the era celebrated their union, even as neither of them seems ever to have considered curtailing his polygamy. Of course, despite—or because of—the surprising success of wives like Nur Jahan, there could be rivalries. In fact, she herself ended up embroiled in controversies and rebellions around the question of succession.

Keeping order became a major preoccupation for Mughal rulers as they expanded across the subcontinent. The Mughal Empire grew exponentially between 1530 and 1707, moving far south into what is now India. When conquered, local rulers often offered their daughters to the Mughal emperor as a sign of peaceful submission. Not all agreed. One experienced woman, Pravin Ray, poet and lover of a defeated raja, refused to leave him and take Emperor Akbar, father of Jahangir, as her new lover, warning Akbar off in mock humility: "Pay heed, wise emperor, to what Pravin Ray has to say. / Only low caste people, crows, and dogs eat off plates used by others."

Rulers faced not only insubordinate women with sharp tongues and pens but also the constant challenge of incorporating a diverse range of people into the Mughal state. The Mughal Empire, like most early modern states, was a growing entity and a process, not a static structure. As in other settings, polygamy

4. This portrait of the exceptional Mughal leader, Nur Jahan, emphasized her enduring loyalty and affection for her recently deceased husband, Emperor Jahangir, whose picture she holds.

helped to suture a complicated, variegated patchwork of an empire. As the Jesuit Jerónimo Xavier noted, Jahangir had married "the daughters of his chief captains and other people, such as petty kings, whom they call Rajas of the gentile caste." Mughals were Sunni, but they chose wives who were Sunni, Shi'a, and even Hindu. These wives helped to broker peaceful alliances throughout the empire. Moreover, they influenced Emperor Akbar, who cut his hair in Hindu fashion, limited his intake of beef, and even seemed to be less reliant on "the friendship of people with beards." The harem was a place to demonstrate the wealth of empire and the strength of its rulers. The Jesuit Xavier was agog at its grandeur: "The opulence of the robes and dresses of this King's wives, as well as gold, silver, jewels, and precious stones is a thing of such astonishment and admiration that it is hard to believe. I refer to the riches not only of the wives, but also of the maids and even the captives."

The splendor of the court and its well-dressed slaves amazed European visitors, one of whom, Francisco Pelsaert, conflated its wealth and women with what he termed "lascivious sensuality, wanton and reckless festivity, superfluous pomp, [and] inflated pride." Yet emperors were expected not to indulge themselves; sexuality was to be used for social and political good, to have children, or to cement alliances. As for Chinese emperors, it was considered weak and unmanly to have sex merely for personal pleasure. Virtue and restraint were necessary for the emperor: for himself, his household, and the empire. Akbar worked hard to secure a reputation for virtue and piety. He regulated the behavior of imperial servants, and he built new structures to ensure the inviolability of his harem. Only he was allowed to visit the women there, and he insisted on their seclusion. His court historian referred to his wives in novel ways, as "cupolas of chastity" and "chaste secluded ladies," so as to emphasize their—and thus the emperor's—purity. He did so even as he flouted traditional Islamic law, which limited the number of wives to four.

Akbar's subversion of laws around polygamy brought him into conflict with his own leading Islamic scholars, too. He instituted public discussions with these scholars to emphasize his own piety and perhaps to emphasize the broad unity of Islam. At one such meeting, he asked the learned men present how many freeborn women a man could legally marry. When they replied four, he asked them what he should do, since he had married more than four. The clerics were unable to agree what the right course of action was, especially given the differences between forms of Islamic domestic partnership, including *mut'ah*, or temporary, marriages, a Shi'ite custom. Akbar then consulted one major cleric who promptly declared that his marriages were not lawful: not the answer Akbar sought. Therefore, Akbar invited comment from various other leading clerics who agreed with his position on the legality of the *mut'ah* marriages. Feeling vindicated, Akbar proceeded to promote these clerics. He kept his multiple wives.

Akbar's disputations with Islamic clerics prefigured those of both himself and his son Jahangir with the Jesuits. Polygamy was a source of controversy there, too. Akbar first encountered the Jesuits in 1573 during a western campaign of conquest. Three of them arrived at his court in 1580. They were taken aback by his polygamy, reporting then that his conversion would be very difficult because "he has so many hobbies and at least a hundred wives." The wives themselves were apparently not keen on his adopting monogamy either. The Jesuits tried to impose Christian monogamy in several missions, first with Akbar and then with his son, Jahangir. The Jesuits claimed that Jahangir accepted some aspects of Christianity, but that he was unwilling to give up his plural wives. He continually badgered the Jesuits about this issue, pointing out the difficulties he would face in doing so. In the end, this disagreement seems to have curtailed Jesuit hopes for his conversion. Despite his evident affection for the exceptional Nur Jahan, Jahangir was no more enthusiastic about monogamy than his father had been, for reasons both personal and political. Polygamy was politically necessary and thus impossible for some rulers to give up, even when clerics, whether Islamic or Christian, argued otherwise.

The complicated interconnections between imperial ambitions and polygamy played out in West African settings, too. As in other areas, missionaries foundered in their attempts to convert leaders to Christian monogamy. There were direct interventions, such as those by Portuguese clergy to convert King Nzinga Nkuwu, the late fifteenth-century ruler of the powerful kingdom of Kongo. He received baptism and seemed to be converted to Christianity, becoming King João I. Nevertheless, within a few years monogamy seemed unworkable for this powerful leader, and he gave up Christianity rather than his wives. Older problematic explanations for this change of heart lay in tired and offensive stereotypes about African lusts; however, it was a political choice. Unlike European systems, in these settings, the sons of the principal wife could not inherit the throne; only the sons of lesser or enslaved wives could do so. To have chosen only one wife would have entirely altered these succession practices and shifted the balance of power among rivals to the throne in dangerous ways. In fact, Afonso, his son by his principal wife, did fight for the throne, supported by his mother, her brother, and Christians who saw him as the rightful heir. Although he had to struggle hard for it, Afonso did manage to become king in 1506. Regardless, in subsequent decades and despite his professed Christianity, he followed traditional practices of polygamy and succession, supporting the sons of his lesser wives in their claims to political power.

Polygamy took on new importance in the realignments of numerous West African kingdoms in the early modern period. For example, in the kingdom of Dahomey, the king lived in a palace populated by what came to be thousands of wives, as well as a much smaller population of eunuchs. This palace complex was at once the household of the king, a city of wives, and the locus of state power and policy decisions. In addition, it came to be the center of a military–state complex. By the 1720s, one

European visitor claimed the king of Dahomey had more than two thousand wives. This number probably rose in the eighteenth century. Yet they were not exactly wives in the usual presumed sense. Probably few of these women were intimate with the king, and certainly only a very limited number had children with him. To be a wife to a king was simply to acknowledge a connection as well as the superiority of his lineage. In the Fon cultures underpinning the kingdom of Dahomey, as in other polygamous cultures, marriage was patrilocal, and a wife, upon moving to her husband's family, divided her loyalty between her own family and that of her husband. When her husband was the king, she was expected to ensure her main loyalty was to his lineage, not her own. So all the women of the palace were technically wives of the king, subordinate to his line. Yet so too were the few men, eunuchs as well as artisans and leaders from recently conquered areas, who lived in the palace complex. All who inhabited the palace, even men, were considered wives of the king because marriage was a metaphor for royal command over all other lineages and thus peoples in the kingdom; rank trumped gender in these marriages.

Marriage in Dahomey integrated a wide cross-section of society, and it also established hierarchies between women. Wives included the wealthy and the noble, free commoners, and captive and enslaved women. Their rank was determined partly by the date of their arrival in the palace. Wealthier families sent their daughters at very young ages so that they could establish a superior position by arriving early. Thus the marriage order could reflect and reinforce rank hierarchies. Yet there was a sense of meritocracy because wives who showed loyalty, competence, and wisdom, or who had favored children, could advance in the palace complex. Wives performed all kinds of roles. Like other Dahomean wives, they labored as farmers and producers of food, as traders and artisans, as healers and ceremonial leaders. Yet beyond these typical wifely roles, wives in the palace also worked as state ministers, civil servants, bureaucrats, soldiers, messengers, and bodyguards.

This extraordinary diversity of wifely roles, as well as the expansion in their numbers, was connected with the expansion of Dahomey itself. Like the empire at Tenochtitlan or that of the Mughals, the empire centered at the palace in Dahomey worked to conquer neighboring areas. In part, Dahomean aims were driven by the overseas slave trade on the coast. There was a defensive element, to protect their own people from the raids of slave traders. Dahomey's expansion likely related to a desire to obtain clear routes to European traders so that they could more easily buy arms, to help in protecting their people from enslavement as well as their own continued growth. The relentless expansion of the slave trade almost certainly led to a series of political and military conquests by Dahomey and to the reshaping of the palace toward further polygyny and an ever-growing number of wives. Even though Europeans sought to end polygamy, their presence here, as elsewhere, may have had the opposite effect.

Dahomey's ability to defend its people depended on this territorial and economic expansion. Its successful defeat of Allada in 1724 added greatly to its holdings and put it finally in the sightline of Europeans, who began to detail its workings, though often with hostility. From 1724 to 1727, the kingdom more than doubled in size, and this conquest came at a cost. Although Dahomey successfully defeated Whydah in 1727, it was plagued by attacks through the late 1720s and into the 1730s. For Dahomey, it was a case of eat or be eaten. It needed to build links, strength, and resources. Wives, some of them originally enslaved, were a chief means of doing so.

Polygyny and the control of the internal slave trade both supported imperial ambitions at Dahomey. It was challenging for the king to maintain control over the enlarged territory, and wives had a vital diplomatic role. As in the Aztec expansion, the center worked to integrate peoples from newly conquered areas, and polygamy was an important way to achieve this integration. Captives could become part of the palace complex and so could daughters sent from conquered local leaders. These women came from outlying areas to join the palace complex as wives, thus ensuring peaceful links between areas. Such women often brought a range of skills and knowledge with them, and they were themselves often extremely successful in wielding power in the kingdom.

One of the most notable ways in which wives showed strength was through their work as armed bodyguards to their husband, the king. The origins of Dahomey women soldiers who became notable figures in subsequent European accounts lay in polygyny itself and the prominent place of women in the palace complex. It was highly unusual for women to control firearms in this era, but wives in Dahomey did so. There was no precedent for this decision, but it led to the establishment of an army of women by the nineteenth century. Wives made political choices in the palace, supporting various factions in terms of succession to the monarchy. Their backing for a particular prince was often the key to his becoming the next king. Wives were critical to the political functioning of state and empire.

Wives demonstrated the wealth and power of the kingdom as well. Often the king met visitors with several of his wives arrayed around him. One traveler reported that the king was surrounded by seven wives, sporting gold rings and bracelets, with necklaces and hair ornaments made of costly beads, who shielded him from the sun with umbrellas, a prestige item. Processions in the palace showed off such grandeur in stunning displays. As one eighteenth-century sojourner, Archibald Dalzel, noted, "The King's seraglio consists of between three and four thousand" wives. Dalzel described one procession that included people bearing expensive and prestigious goods, including arms, umbrellas, and gold. It began with more than one hundred male guards, all carrying guns. There followed fifteen of his daughters, attended by fifty enslaved women. Then came over seven hundred wives, bearing provisions and liquor. Then came another ninety wives, all armed, with drums. Then followed more wives and children and eunuchs, some of them passing out gifts or giving speeches in praise of the king. It was an astonishing display of royal power, and it depended largely on the wives of the palace.

Wives showed a royal dynasty's wealth and strength; they brokered power in palaces, which were the main locus of state power in the early modern era. Although Europeans wanted leading men to give up their plural wives, the realignments of the early modern era, partly related to European expansion, meant that they were not always eager to do so. The wives themselves may not have always welcomed these changes, as a few hints from

5. This drawing depicts the king of Dahomey going to war, followed by armed wives. It was highly unusual for women to carry firearms. This army of women, along with the use of umbrellas, a high-prestige item, and the bystanders kowtowing on the ground as they pass, demonstrate both the power and the wealth of this kingdom.

the Mughal Empire imply. Even when wives preferred monogamy, it may have had as much to do with novel structures of law, inheritance, and economics as with the activities of missionaries. Throughout all of these settings, polygamy became a point of contention, a source of "difficulties": between wives and husbands, between rulers and clerics, between colonizers and indigenous rulers.

Chapter 4
Protestantism

Perversion, Protestantism, poison, and polygamy all seemed to come together in the German-speaking city of Münster in the 1520s. In a salacious and lengthy report, one Catholic historian and teacher, Hermann von Kerssenbrock, painted a vivid picture of the scandalous behavior of the radical Protestant reformers there who had overthrown the authorities and taken over the city. In von Kerssenbrock's account, nuns, casting off their habits, ran wanton, making "use of this opportunity to ruin themselves"; orgies took place nightly. One "woman of outstanding beauty and peaceful disposition" apparently even created a poisoned pair of underpants to give to the Catholic bishop to murder him. In this febrile atmosphere, polygamy was only one of the numerous outrages perpetuated at Münster. It was an important one, though, revealing much about the controversies generated by the reconfiguration of marriage at the heart of the Protestant Reformation. The very name of this city would come to stand in for reform run amok.

According to their enemies, the leaders of the Münster rebellion took plural wives, thus ensuring that many Europeans came to conflate polygamy and radical Protestantism. The shocking events in Münster worried authorities, both Catholic and Protestant, because they recognized that the adoption of polygamy was rooted in theological justifications as well as in social reform. As von

Kerssenbrock put it, "being themselves devoted to lechery and impudence, [the rebels] readily decided that by the example of Abraham, Jacob, David, and the other patriarchs of the Old Testament ... it was permissible to have several wives." These Protestants evidently emulated the ancient patriarchs, and they wanted to grow their population, in a city with a considerable majority of women. Von Kerssenbrock claimed that leaders believed "that it was sinful to waste semen.... Therefore ... whenever they have a pregnant or infertile wife, they are allowed to marry another." They also sought to make marriage holier, unsullied by the usual practical considerations of advancement or physical attraction. The Münster rebels contended that "since all marriages had been contracted not according to the Spirit but for the sake of appearance or beauty or money or wealth or having grander relations," they rejected these contracts and instead "performed the marriages anew." Marriage, including polygamy, was to be more pious, purer, better.

In Münster, the local Catholic bishop (who had wisely refused the poisoned underpants) joined with local princes and other towns to end the Protestant takeover, determined "not to allow a new Turkish kingdom to take root in the middle of Christendom." Anxieties about Muslim marriage practices took on new force in the sixteenth century, as the Ottoman Empire was in ascendance and knocked on the gates of Vienna. Stories of the outrages perpetuated at Münster circulated widely in Europe and beyond. To their enemies, these committed Protestants at Münster were like the woman who made the toxic undergarments for the bishop: all too liable to contaminate Catholics in ways that were below the belt. Eager to discredit reformers, Catholics used the tale of Münster as a warning to others of what might happen if Protestantism were allowed to flourish unchecked. One critic claimed that "everyone is saying that you Lutherans want to carry on like the Turks and the Münsterites." If theological reform went too far, it might end up in the kind of uncontrolled behavior that seemed to be on show in Münster. More moderate Protestants worried about these discrediting excesses.

Although Münster stood as an outlier even for the vast majority of Protestants, a few Protestants, far less radical, did indeed envision a new world of marriage. The rethinking of marriage and the household and the weighting of Old Testament examples were common to Protestants of all stripes. Protestants rejected the Catholic definition of marriage as a sacrament, opening the door to shifting marriage from a religious act to a civil one, to be regulated by secular authorities and increasingly powerful nation-states. At the same time, though, the rejection of clerical marriage meant that even the holiest Christian could, and should, now be married; celibacy was no longer the highest ideal for Christians. Instead, for Protestants, marriage was to anchor new forms of household piety as well as bodily and social discipline; it was the only way to ensure a holy household.

In every century from the sixteenth on, this reform of marriage at the heart of Protestant thinking has given rise to Protestants arguing in favor of polygamy. As a number of them noted, Old Testament patriarchs, considered holy and beloved by God, practiced polygamy. The emphasis on the return to Old Testament examples and the word of God meant that these ancient polygamists loomed larger for Protestants than they did for Catholics. At the same time, there was no explicit condemnation of polygamy in the New Testament, and a variety of Protestant thinkers wondered whether its renunciation was, like clerical marriage, a later, corrupt Catholic teaching. For at least a few Protestants, polygamy has seemed a natural extension of this celebration of holy marriage (over celibacy), to contain dangerous lusts and to ensure emulation of the holy patriarchs of the Old Testament such as Abraham. If it meant that all women became wives, then so much the better for society, at least according to a range of reformers and thinkers from Münster on.

Two sixteenth-century controversies involving the complicated marital and inheritance needs of two rulers, Henry VIII of England and Philip, Landgrave of Hesse, led a few notable Protestant reformers to consider polygamy seriously. Both of these rulers seemed for many years unable to sire a male heir, and this problem had implications for their realms. Therefore, their domestic challenges became grave matters of state and church, as a variety of leaders struggled to figure out the best way to mitigate the crises provoked by this lack of male heirs. A number of leading theologians across Europe posited that it would be better for Henry VIII to adopt bigamy than to divorce Catherine of Aragon. In 1531, Martin Luther even advised one Englishman that although divine law forbad divorce, the example of Old Testament patriarchs meant that perhaps the king could marry another woman. Similar issues arose for Philip of Hesse. In this case, a number of prominent reformers, including Luther, Philip Melanchthon, Martin Bucer, and others, published a statement that effectively left the decision over bigamy to Philip's own conscience, thus opening the door to plural marriage. Admittedly, these reformers may have agreed to this elite polygamy out of political expediency, eager to keep on the good side of rulers and certainly only permitting polygamy in exceptional circumstances for exceptional men. Nevertheless, these moments suggested that even Christian Protestant kings might take plural wives.

Early modern Protestant intellectuals pondered polygamy, too, cautious but willing to consider it. One Protestant who fled Italy, Bernardino Ochino, penned a dialogue on polygamy of an unhappily married man with a barren wife seeking advice from his friend as to whether polygamy might be a solution. Ochino underscored the precedent of Old Testament polygamy as well as the general silence about it in the New Testament and early Christian writings. He stressed that polygamy might have social advantages: solving infertility, lack of population growth, and disorders associated with adultery, prostitution, and fornication. As in most early modern tracts on polygamy, condemnation was reserved for the possibility that a woman might have multiple husbands, not for a man having multiple wives. Although by the conclusion Ochino explicitly rejected polygyny (with the frustrated husband simply advised to pray for "the gift of continence"), in fact the treatise alludes to its possible benefits. Even more explicit support for polygamy occurs in the seventeenth-century writings of a German reformer, Johannes Leyser, who outlined the theological justifications for polygamy as well as its domestic and social advantages.

Those "hotter" Protestants called "Puritans" wondered over polygamy and especially the problem of Old Testament patriarchs who practiced it. They too saw the story of Adam and Eve as proof that God had made one woman for one man and that marriage made them one flesh, thus ensuring human monogamy. As one divine put it, "Polygamie is contrary to the first institution of God, for God made one man and one woman, and not one man and two women." This foundational argument from Adam and Eve's union echoed through a number of writings, just as it had in the late antique and medieval eras among Catholic theologians. There was emphasis on an injunction in Leviticus (18:27) ordering that a man should not take a sister as a plural wife. Most authors agreed that this rule was not a prohibition against literal sisters, but against the taking of multiple women as wives.

Those reformers who rejected polygamy usually added a range of other arguments against it, but the issue and especially the Old Testament examples of plural marriages gnawed at them. William Ames, a Cambridge-educated reformer popular in seventeenth-century England and New England, upheld the Adam and Eve story as a key precedent. He contended that polygamy destroyed marital affections, family peace, and good parenting. In addition, he looked to nature: if birds could manage monogamy, then surely human beings should be able to match them. Yet reformers such as Ames always faced this problem: the Old Testament contained numerous examples of holy patriarchs, beloved by God, who had practiced polygamy. Like other thinkers, he decided that these ancient men must have had some kind of "dispensation." Another reforming divine, John Weemes, stacked up reasons relating to nature and society, contending that the lack of any recorded polyandry in human history meant that polygyny, too, was unacceptable. He claimed that for the ancient Jews, polygamy had been merely a sin of ignorance. Yet, he asserted, if a man knew it was wrong, as modern Christians did, it became adultery, pure and simple. One New England minister, John Cotton, dismissed the polygamy of Old Testament figures as a sin of ignorance: acceptable only when men did not know it was a sin. For Cotton, modern Christians, aware that polygamy was a sin, could not therefore practice it.

One Protestant thinker and poet who refused to condemn Old Testament polygamy was John Milton. Despite his memorable portrait of the monogamy of Adam and Eve in *Paradise Lost*, he made a case for both polygamy and divorce. He died before he could publish his incendiary views on polygamy, but he wrote elaborate theological justifications in his work *On Christian Doctrine*. The idea that *only* two should become one flesh held no weight for him. Milton contended that the polygamy of the blessed patriarchs demonstrated its righteousness: "Polygamy is either marriage or else it is whoredom or adultery....Let no one dare to say that it is whoredom or adultery—respect for so many polygamous patriarchs will, as I hope, stop him!" Those patriarchs whom God "loved supremely" could not be dismissed as "whoremongers and adulterers," their progeny rejected as "bastards." For Milton, the piety of these men and their offspring proved that polygamy was no sin. After all, how could it be that "so many men of the highest rank sinned throughout so many centuries" or that "God would have endured it in his own people?" Milton stressed the silence of most of the rest of the Bible: "Absolutely no trace of the reproving of polygamy is seen in the whole law." There was also no general condemnation in the New Testament, a point to which later defenders would return.

One eighteenth-century bishop, Gilbert Burnet, claimed in the 1730s that there might be some good in systems of polygamy, although there may have been a satirical slant to his work. Still, he refuted men like Ames by asserting that polygamy was not against the laws of marriage or of nature. He highlighted the Ottoman Turks as a powerful empire prospering in part thanks to polygamy. He noted its presence among Old Testament patriarchs, and he observed that there was no condemnation of it in the New Testament. Another divine, Patrick Delany, declared in the 1730s, likely with some exaggeration, that "polygamy is a doctrine daily defended in common conversation, and often in print, by a great variety of *plausible* arguments." Delaney attacked it in a tract of two hundred pages, stressing that it violated the natural order and led to domestic discord, the neglect of children, and a range of social ills. Delaney was notable in singling out the harm to women, an increasing point of discussion in the eighteenth century, pointing to "the miserable state of servitude to which the whole female world are reduced" wherever polygamy occurred. Delaney underscored that polygamy destroyed "the natural equality of desire" established to ensure the continuation of the human species, resulting in "the detestable evils of Sodomy and Eviration [loss of masculinity]." These kinds of criticisms would continue to be made into the modern era.

Nevertheless, other eighteenth-century Protestant writers were more favorable toward polygamy, including the Reverend Martin Madan, a Methodist-leaning minister and former barrister, who in 1780 in London published *Thelyphthora, or a Treatise on Female Ruin*, a two-volume treatise (later expanded to three volumes) calling for the reform of marriage law in England, including the legalization of polygyny. Madan's unusual remedy for social and sexual disorder was to require that a man consider himself married to any unmarried woman with whom he had sex. Madan thus defined marriage as the carnal union of man and unmarried woman and claimed that, were such intercourse recognized as the divine form of marriage, "no *brothels* would teem with harlots—no streets swarm with *prostitutes.... Adultery* and *whoredom* would no longer dare to face the light." Madan assumed that men would find it difficult to remain faithful to a single woman. He targeted situations in which wives were infertile, ill, or had bad or flighty tempers. Madan suggested that in such cases men (and men only—on this point, he was unequivocal) should be allowed more than one wife. Madan pursued these points with biblical interpretation relying on his knowledge of Hebrew, Latin, and Greek; the examples of the Old Testament patriarchs loomed large in his discussion.

Thelyphthora provoked an outpouring of reviews and countertreatises, newspaper notices, poems, plays, and popular prints. The topic became a staple of London debating societies. As one newspaper critic observed, "Witness the infinite letters, epigrams, and lampoons, in almost every news-paper, on this subject; witness the public disputations in places of amusement." Madan's proposals touched raw nerves in English society in this era, including ongoing unease about the exploitations of women, especially poor ones who turned to prostitution. Madan contended that, in his system, "millions of women (especially of the lower sort) would be saved from ruin."

There was a vigorous response to Madan's treatise as critics of various stripes, including fellow Methodists, rushed to denounce these heterodox notions. Polygamy would surely lead to jealousy among women, resentments, and domestic discord. One satirical poem, attributed to "Mohammed the Prophet" (clearly a false pen name for a scurrilous anonymous poem, likely published in 1782), claimed that through Madan, Islamic ideas would infiltrate England: so that Madan would give "new *Korans* in *Thelyphthora*." For the audience for such satires, these references signaled the kind of imagined social and political tyranny "of the East" to be rejected in England. One newspaper mockingly reported that a group of five hundred women rioted against Madan, burning him in effigy after denouncing his attempts to keep them in a "Turkish seraglio." Here were echoes of claims that Münster rebels wished to set up a "Turkish kingdom" in the middle of Christian Europe. Other critics condemned Madan for implying that a man with a troublesome wife should be allowed to take another, rather than working for greater domestic harmony.

The published tracts and reviews castigating Madan were penned by men, but there is some record of responses from women. One prominent Methodist patron, the countess of Huntingdon, instigated a petition that gained more than three thousand signatures to try to stop Madan from publishing his treatise in the first place (he did anyway). Polygamy became a major topic for debating societies in London in 1780–81; women attended many of these debates. One all-female debating society pondered, "Can the Rev. Mr. Madan's doctrine of plurality of wives be justified by the laws of policy or religion?" Though an assembly of men rejected Madan's polygamy in debate, an assembly of women had endorsed it. Other women wrote their friends in consternation, impressed by Madan's sympathy for suffering women but worried by the implications of his radical reform plan.

Such debates over polygamy were not restricted to England. In 1780, a New England church excommunicated one member, John Miner, who had publicly defended polygamy. Miner went into print to vindicate himself and to prove why polygamy was theologically and socially justified. God could have spoken against it and yet never did, he wrote, nor had Jesus himself. Miner underlined the social advantages of polygamy and the ways it could support well-ordered families. He enumerated its practical benefits, especially useful when there was a preponderance of females, as in times of war. While he conceded that plural unions might lead to disputes between wives, such was no reason to forbid the practice. By the same logic, he reasoned, families should not have more than one child, since siblings argued, too.

Propolygamy ideas thus circulated in the English-speaking world in the late eighteenth century. Some of these ideas found fertile soil in the zealous Protestant utopianism of the early nineteenth-century United States. In the 1810s, radical reformer Jacob Cochran founded a movement in Maine that recast marriage into what he believed to be holier and better forms. As with Münster, our sources about this program and sect mostly come from enemies, so it is difficult to know exactly what the "Cochranites" believed or practiced. One hostile account declared that "each Brother & Sister in this fraternity has his Spiritual Wife, Mate or yokefelow." This system of "spiritual wifery," which may have included polygamy, shocked outsiders, with tales of the "lascivious behavior" and "all manner of iniquity" of the novel communities circulating in local newspapers. The movement collapsed when Jacob Cochran was convicted of "lewdness" in 1819.

Other groups of zealous spiritualists who rethought marital arrangements included the Shakers, an Anglo-American group that rejected marriage altogether but lived in "family order" in communal groups bound by spiritual, rather than legal or blood, ties. They also included John Humphrey Noyes, who founded the Oneida community in upstate New York in 1848, and his followers. At Oneida, Noyes instituted a system of "complex marriage" in which individuals moved between sexual partners. All were to live in the community, without the monogamy that Noyes criticized as "selfish." Men were expected to practice continence, avoiding ejaculation, but any children born were to be raised communally.

These experiments in spiritual wifery, novel domestic orders, and complex marriages may be seen as yet another set of branches of a large and long-rooted tree of the Protestant recasting of marriage, starting with those reviled rebels at Münster. For all of these Protestants, marriage was an important arena for religious and social reform, with theological justifications for polygamy firmly in place in centuries of writing and thinking about it. Like those sixteenth-century reformers in Münster, nineteenth-century Americans continued to envision new worlds of marriage, ones supporting the spiritual and domestic ambitions of reformed Christians. One of the most creative and energetic of these reformers was Joseph Smith, a farmer from upstate New York who became the founder of the group called the Mormons. His embrace of a novel theology of marriage, which included polygamy, put this form at the center of conflicts that would reverberate throughout the modern era.

Chapter 5
Mormonism

"That a new era for woman has commenced here in America and elsewhere is positive and apparent. From nearly all quarters of the globe come the tidings of woman's advancement." So declared a triumphant American newspaper editorial in 1877. Its author, Emmeline B. Wells, was writing in Salt Lake City, Utah, where she was the editor of the *Woman's Exponent* and a representative for Utah Territory at the National Woman Suffrage Convention. In addition, Emmeline Wells was the seventh wife of a local Mormon leader and the mother of six children.

For a plural wife and polygamy advocate to laud women's global achievements in a newspaper edited and run by women might seem surprising, when most Americans considered such wives to be mere dupes of patriarchal oppression and domestic tyranny. Nevertheless, Mormon plural wives such as Emmeline Wells did not accept this characterization, despite the outrage they occasioned. This same newspaper had noted five years earlier that "great outcry is raised against the much marrying of the Latter-day Saints." Polygamy came to take on particular and highly visible national importance in the United States in the nineteenth century. Although Mormons asserted, as Wells did in 1879, that "the polygamy of Utah is doing no harm to the United States," few Americans agreed. The government of the United States worked hard to end polygamy in Utah and elsewhere. As in other times

C. M. Bell, WASHINGTON. D. C.

6. This photo shows Emmeline Wells in her early sixties, when she was the established editor of the *Woman's Exponent* as well as a national campaigner for woman's suffrage. The picture was taken a year after the Woodruff Manifesto had discouraged Mormons from contracting plural marriages.

and places, for many nineteenth-century Americans, polygamy, like slavery, demarcated barbaric despotism from civility, progress, and republicanism. Mormons, of course, rejected these associations.

What is now the Church of Jesus Christ of Latter-day Saints (LDS) began when Joseph Smith gathered converts in upstate New York in 1830. Its core sacred text was the Book of Mormon, which resulted from prophecies Smith received in the 1820s. That text told a tale of continued revelation in ancient America in a set of stories reminiscent of the Old Testament. It was a revolutionary Protestantism with millennial expectations and an alternative version of ancient history, one that ran alongside the Bible but added new sacred texts. Americans of this era, often dissatisfied with staid older forms of religion, found this lively new American-based theology, with its prospect of modern revelations and prophets, appealing, and so others joined the charismatic Smith. In the fervid atmosphere of utopianism of the early nineteenth-century United States, and with an early missionary impulse, the church experienced considerable growth. The Saints, as they called themselves, provoked angry reactions as they preached and formed novel communities under the leadership of the inspiring, but controversial, Smith. It was this radical theology and formation of a new and competing church and tradition, not polygamy, that provoked American aggression. However, in the end, the belief in, and practices of, plural marriage exacerbated this hostility against the Mormons. As in Münster, enemies of Mormons used its commitment to reimagined forms of marriage to condemn and discredit the movement as a whole.

In 1840, Joseph Smith began revealing to his closest supporters his innovative theology of marriage, which included the possibility of spouses being married "for time and eternity." This form of "celestial marriage" was one part of a profound recasting of marriage and family in LDS theology. Marriage became a necessary step to salvation for women and men, everlasting if sealed by the proper authorities. There could be marriages on earth ("for time"), marriages to those already gone ("for eternity"), and marriages recognized both on earth and in heaven ("for time and eternity"). Celestial marriages were considered the most elevated type. "The Principle" of plural marriage allowed a man to take multiple wives.

By 1842, rumors were already swirling about Smith's plural marriages. One critic, John Bennett Cook, published an exposé of Smith and his "spiritual wifery." Here again, charges of polygamy, and of alleged domestic and sexual disorder, were ways to discredit a religious radical. Still, in this case, there was some truth to the scandalous stories. Smith was beginning to put into practice his new forms of marriage, including polygamy. He was married monogamously to Emma Smith, but, in 1841, he married other women, too. It has been a source of considerable debate among the faithful as to whether Smith married women who were married to other men. It does seem to be the case that he contracted a number of different types of marriages, often involving women who did not live with him. Given the secrecy surrounding them, it is difficult to know what exactly took place in terms of these marriages. Yet, regardless of this uncertainty, plural marriage for Smith and others meant multiple wives, not husbands, and it came to be a foundational aspect of nineteenth-century Mormon patriarchal principles.

Joseph Smith's adoption of plural marriage was extremely controversial, even among his nearest and dearest. His wife, Emma, resisted this new doctrine. Following prolonged quarrels with her, he evidently received an important revelation. In Chapter 132 of the Doctrine and Covenants, a book of teachings of the LDS Church, the theology of celestial marriage took shape, promising rewards in heaven for those who pursued the path of celestial marriage. This chapter upheld the examples of Old Testament polygamists, Abraham, Solomon, and David. Such men were models of righteous marriage even in modern times. This section laid out the "law of Sarah," in which the first wife was supposed to give permission for subsequent wives, just as Sarah had enjoined Abraham to take Hagar as a secondary wife. It was possible for a man to gain exemption from this law of Sarah, but on the whole, the ideal was that an existing wife should approve the taking of additional wives. Emma Smith never welcomed this move, eventually leading public campaigns against polygamy.

Divisions over polygamy erupted as soon as plural marriages started among the Mormons, sometimes even in the same household, as well as in the larger community. Joseph Smith and the Mormons had long faced critical responses, well before polygamy started. They sought refuge first in various places in Missouri, but to no avail. Then they set up a community in Nauvoo, Illinois. They stayed there for some years, but then Smith was arrested and subsequently lynched by an angry mob in the jail where he was held in Carthage, Illinois, in 1844. At this point, the Mormons had to flee Illinois, too. Well before his death, Joseph Smith had set up a Quorum of Twelve Apostles to help lead the church; it included men such as Brigham Young and brothers Orson and Parley Pratt, who had already begun to practice plural marriage before Smith's death.

Smith's murder by a mob in 1844 reinforced the importance of plural marriage. In addition to its theological centrality, polygamy took on political and social significance. There was no clear successor to Smith, and in part, men who followed his practice of plural marriage were claiming they were his spiritual heirs. There was a flurry of plural marriages after Smith's demise, with Young, for instance, taking ten new wives in the autumn of 1844. Some of these wives were Smith's widows. When Brigham Young assumed the mantle of leadership and led the Mormons to Utah in the 1840s, he was the husband of multiple women and the father of multiple children. He was not alone in this respect. By 1846, as the Saints began their arduous journey west, polygamy had become an open secret as more and more families adopted it.

Prior to their departure, more than two hundred men and seven hundred women, close to 8 percent of the Mormon population, were living in plural unions.

In 1852, from their new community in Salt Lake City, the leaders of the LDS Church publicly acknowledged plural marriage as a theological principle. At a special conference of church elders, publicized in their newspaper, the *Deseret News*, the doctrine of plural marriage received public endorsement, announced by Orson Pratt, one of the Quorum. He observed that four-fifths of people around the world allowed polygamy. He asserted that such people were in fact more enlightened than modern Americans and Europeans. He upheld the example of the ancient patriarchs such as Abraham and Jacob.

Why did LDS men adopt polygamy? Why did LDS women? Most fundamentally, plural marriage held profound theological significance as a path to salvation. At its height, many Mormons considered that celestial marriage allowed for a higher level of eternal life. Brigham Young even contended that "the only men who become Gods, even the Sons of God, are those who enter into polygamy.'" For Young, not everyone needed to *practice* it "to obtain the blessings which Abraham obtained," but everyone needed to believe in it. For both women and men, it was a way to bring new souls into the world, to raise "a royal Priesthood, a peculiar people," as Young put it. The descendants of Abraham should multiply and replenish the earth, and polygamy seemed to support such a vision of population growth. One leader, George Q. Cannon, preached in 1869 that basic physical passions had been given both to women and to men in order to populate the earth and to bring forth souls in married unions. Even women's quilts sewn by plural wives celebrated fecundity in LDS communities.

Moreover, plural marriages established lineage with, and devotion to, Joseph Smith. Of those appointed to leadership positions from

1845 to 1888, nearly 70 percent had multiple wives. As in other settings, plural marriages showed the ability of powerful men to support a large family. Polygamy thus had political, social, and economic resonance. It gave men new partners and new household laborers; a number of the wives were younger than their husbands. In 1844, one of forty-three-year-old Brigham Young's wives was sixteen and another was seventeen, though most were in their twenties and thirties, even forties. In the settling of Utah, in particular, this household labor was crucial, and many men, away on missions, relied on the industry and productivity of their wives and children. Orson Pratt, Brigham Young, and others were quick to repudiate the notion that plural marriage was "a doctrine...to gratify the carnal lusts and feelings of man," but their enemies tended to believe otherwise.

For the women, the equation was different. Yet they too felt that celestial marriage brought rewards in the afterlife. Here on earth, polygamy was sometimes a way to depart a bad marriage (to a less than ideal first husband) or to surmount a vulnerable widowhood with children. It could offer security and stability. It was a way to connect to a powerful man and to join an established family and network. Many LDS plural wives in Utah had been widowed, divorced, or fatherless, so plural marriage gave them a chance to find a household and a more protected situation. Yet there was usually resistance, especially in the first generation. Some of the "first wives" like Emma Smith were unhappy about new wives added to what had been a traditional monogamous marriage. For example, Parley Pratt had a monogamous wife, Mary Ann, whom he married when his first wife died, who eventually left him when he started adding plural wives to the household.

This issue about divorce flags a critical feature of Mormon marriage systems: divorce was allowed. The church regulated both marriage and divorce, and it was more willing to grant divorces, especially on the basis of women's unhappiness, than most American states were in this period. Utah ecclesiastical courts allowed divorce from the start, and Utah Territory passed a law in 1852 permitting divorce for a range of reasons, including relations that lacked "peace and union" in the home. Although Brigham Young disliked divorce, he presided over many of them. His clerk noted that he "never refuses to grant a bill [of divorce] on the application of the wife, and NEVER when she INSISTS on it." Plural wives were not forced to stay, and some left unhappy marriages. The ways in which plural marriage and divorce co-existed can be seen in the tumultuous married life of Brigham Young's "adopted" son, John Doyle Lee. Of his fourteen wives, two died and seven left him.

The LDS marriage structure was thus a system with some agency for individuals, including wives. The ideal was that husbands had approval from existing wives to add another one to the family, the law of Sarah. Belinda Pratt, the sister-in-law of Orson and wife of Parley, both polygamous leaders of the church, wrote a treatise defending polygamy in 1854. She emphasized women's agency in the system. She pointed to the Old Testament, terming the "honorable and virtuous" Sarah "a pattern for Christian ladies to imitate." Belinda Pratt herself had fled an unhappy first monogamous marriage to a lapsed Mormon in Boston, and she became one of the generation who went to Utah to settle their families. She lived in polygamy for several years until widowed, and she remained a vocal defender of this principle to the end of her days in the 1890s.

As with all marriages, whether monogamous or polygamous, some LDS marriages were happier than others. Relations between spouses could range from loving to angry. Outsiders assumed that it was a system in which wives endured endless jealousy and resentment, but it was not always so. One visitor to Salt Lake City in 1857 noted, "The wretchedness of wives in Utah has been greatly exaggerated." A plural wife had to work with other wives and their children, as well as with their husband and own children. In the hardscrabble years of exile and settlement in

Utah, resources were limited. Husbands were often away for work or on missions. As one sympathetic visitor reported in 1852, "That the wives find the relation often a lonesome and burdensome one, is certain; though usually the surface of society wears a smiling countenance." Some wives lived separately, which could smooth tensions but exacerbate loneliness. Sometimes they shared houses, which could increase rivalries over resources. Even Emmeline Wells, who publicly defended plural marriage, suffered when her husband lost his fortune and, while she was away, sold her house of thirty-seven years. She loved her home and garden, and she felt bereft when they were sold without her knowledge or permission. Still, this situation was not about polygamy itself, but rather about the way husbands were allowed to behave—and sometimes did—under American law.

Wives, often firm in their faith, tried hard to endure polygamy's challenges, but sometimes they found it nearly impossible. One first wife expressed her chagrin by throwing a shoe through a second wife's window. She ended up seeking a divorce, as did a number of plural wives. In 1866, one husband in Provo, Utah, decided to add a second wife to his family. His first wife believed in plural marriage and so she tried to manage. For some months, the two wives got along fine. Yet the house, with two wives and ever more children, became cramped. Work on a second house commenced. In the meantime, the second wife's family came to stay, exacerbating tensions. Divorce was the result. Another Utah wife declared flatly, "There is no such thing as happiness...where a man has more than one" wife.

Yet other Mormon plural wives found shared labor, child care, and support invaluable. The work of three wives, Henny, Elizabeth, and Martha, in the household of Isaiah Cox in 1880 made the house an orderly place, even with fourteen lively children, ranging in age from one to twenty-one. The whole family woke early for labor and prayer. One wife did the cooking and kitchen work, another made the beds and swept, and the third washed and dressed the children. Thanks to their efforts, by 7:30 everyone was ready for breakfast. On weekly wash days, everyone pitched in. Rarely did all the wives go out together, even to church, as someone usually had to stay home to take care of the children. The wives helped each other in childbirth and swapped maternity and baby clothes. One wife, Martha Cox, was able to teach school because another wife looked after her children. Doubtless, there were tensions. Still, in the 1920s, Martha Cox termed her sister-wives "the two best women in the world," observing that "we three…loved each other more than sisters." Childcare shared between wives even allowed a few plural wives to pursue unusual levels of professional advancement, as for Ellis Shipp who left her three children with sister-wives to attend the Women's Medical College in Philadelphia. When she returned to Salt Lake City, Shipp founded Utah's School of Nursing and Obstetrics, something that would have been virtually impossible had other wives not given their support along the way.

The place of women in Mormon plural marriages has prompted debates about the effects of polygamy. Was it oppressive or liberating? It was both. It was undeniably patriarchal and often restrictive, yet it could create spaces for female solidarity and even self-fulfillment. Martha Hughes Cannon, a doctor who became the first woman state senator (beating her own husband in the election), contended in the 1890s that, without needing to attend to a husband every day, "a plural wife has more time to herself and more independence every way than a single one." Yet in private, Martha Hughes Cannon raged when her husband took another wife driving in a fancy carriage while she herself endured financial privations. So there was never total unanimity about polygamy, even sometimes in the same household or for the same individuals. Moreover, supporting the Principle of plural marriage did not mean that individual wives were not sometimes unhappy with their husbands or resentful of other wives. We should be careful, though, of laying all the blame for unhappiness with polygamy, since there were numerous unhappy monogamous marriages in the nineteenth-century United States, too. Nineteenth-century marriage law throughout the United States favored men, and women lost property and rights on entering marriage, whether single or plural.

Some wives at least publicly supported plural marriage; others made their unhappiness clear. But to most non-Mormons, it did not matter if women seemed to accept polygamy; the assumption was that they must have been tricked and seduced into becoming plural wives. Polygamy seemed perverse to outsiders, and Americans associated it with barbarism and despotism. Several antipolygamy novels gained widespread readerships in the 1850s: Maria Ward's *Female Life among the Mormons* (1855), Metta Victoria Fuller's *Mormon Wives* (1856), Orvilla Belisle's *Mormonism Unveiled* (1855), and Alfreda Eva Bell's *Boadicea* (1855). The authors of such novels depicted Utah as a wicked place where women lived in "harems" and "seraglios," presided over by despotic husbands who acted like Turkish tyrants. Such works connected polygamy and slavery, making the point that both were situations in which tyrants abused and oppressed cowering subordinates. Antislavery, a major cause in the mid-nineteenth-century United States, influenced antipolygamy. Over the ensuing fifty years, one hundred novels and countless magazine and newspaper stories continued to tell antipolygamy tales. They struck a chord. In the 1880s, one young reader, on finishing an antipolygamy novel, declared with earnest resolution, "If I should ever become a statesman, I will dedicate myself to exterminating this curse."

Such novels, as well as first-person accounts from Utah, combined to suggest that tyranny, violence, and trouble attended the domestic practices of Mormons. In one of the most vituperative travel accounts, published in 1854, Benjamin G. Ferris announced that polygamy, "the offspring of lust," was incompatible with national strength and prosperity and thus dangerous to the larger American body politic, just as slavery was. He connected plural marriages with racial degeneracy. "It belongs now to the indolent and opium-eating Turks and Asiatics, the miserable Africans, the North American savages, and the Latter-day Saints," averred Ferris, lumping together a variety of practices into one unholy global mess. In a first-person account, one of Brigham Young's aggrieved former wives, Ann Eliza Young, painted a vivid picture of Mormon polygamy, which, she contended, was "reeking…with filth and moral poison; rotten to the very core; a leprous spot on the body politic." She lamented that women were the greatest sufferers, but she also decried the moral decay of men who "lose manliness, and descend to the level of brutes."

The linkage of polygamy with emasculation and racial degeneracy became a popular trope of antipolygamy. One hostile observer of the Mormons claimed that polygamy left its mark "in the genital weakness of the boys and young men" and their general infertility. This reporter went even further, declaring that the physical effects of polygamy had transformed Mormons into a distinct and debauched race: "The yellow, sunken, cadaverous visage; the greenish-colored eyes; the thick, protuberant lips; the low forehead, the light, yellowish hair; and the lank, angular person, constitute an appearance so characteristic of the new race, the production of polygamy, as to distinguish them at a glance." Even a more restrained account, by the political theorist Francis Lieber, traced out the racial disparities of people with differing marriage systems. He asserted that monogamy "is one of the elementary distinctions…between European and Asiatic humanity…one of the pre-existing conditions of our existence as civilized white men." He warned, "Strike it out, and you destroy our very being, and when we say *our*, we mean our race."

Politicians were quick to join this antipolygamy chorus. Critics linked plural marriage with barbaric practices of slavery, both to be excised from the body politic. "Point me to a nation where polygamy is practiced," demanded one congressional representative in 1854, "and I will point you to heathens and barbarians. It seriously affects the prosperity of States, it retards civilization, it uproots Christianity." Why, he enquired, should the US government send funding to Utah to pay "for the debauching of our daughters and the deluding of our wives?" Such denunciations filled congressional debates in the 1850s and early 1860s. Justin Morrill, a Vermont congressman, was a Republican reformer and abolitionist; he led the charge against polygamy in Utah Territory. In 1857, Morrill fretted that polygamy ruined the equality that should be the foundation of marriage, so that men became despots and women were debased, just as slavery perverted social relations. The Republican Party had included the eradication of plural marriages in its party platform of 1856, promising to rid the American territories of "those twin relics of barbarism—Polygamy, and Slavery." Ending both enhanced federal powers and showed how progressive Americans were. Morrill was successful in getting the Morrill Anti-Bigamy Act passed and signed into law by Abraham Lincoln in 1862. The law banned plural marriage in federal territories, though it was not well enforced. Slavery in the United States was legally ended by 1865.

In the aftermath of the Civil War, Mormons, largely left to build their own communities in Utah in the 1860s, were sufficiently confident about the nonenforcement of this antibigamy law that they decided to pursue a test case. George Reynolds was Brigham Young's secretary, and he had been prosecuted for being married to two women. He brought a case against the US government in hopes of overturning federal antipolygamy laws. Mormons argued that, as plural marriage was an essential part of their beliefs, they should be allowed to marry plural wives because the First Amendment protected the right to practice one's religion freely.

The Supreme Court did not agree with this reasoning. In a landmark decision, *Reynolds v. United States* (1879), it declared that polygamy, threatening to civilization itself, was so incompatible with the American republic that they could not coexist, even if belief in the sanctity of plural marriages was part of Mormon theology. The Supreme Court made this ruling in the wake of a civil war that had pointed up the need for federal powers to end barbaric practices like slavery. The Supreme Court stressed the foundational nature of monogamy: "Upon it society may be said to be built." Using the theories of Lieber and others, the court declared that "polygamy has always been odious among the northern and western nations of Europe, and, until the establishment of the Mormon Church, was almost exclusively a feature of the life of Asiatic and of African people."

Legislation followed the Supreme Court decision, making life for Utah's polygamists more and more difficult. The Edmunds Act of 1882 and the Edmunds–Tucker Act of 1887 prescribed escalating penalties against polygamy to deprive Mormon polygamist husbands of rights and property. Inheritance by wives and children in plural marriage situations became more difficult as well. Enforcement of these laws began in earnest. Federal authorities prosecuted polygamy under various guises, as American law recognized no wives beyond the first one. They often went after husbands with multiple wives on the basis of illegal "cohabitation" with more than one woman. From 1882, there were more than 1,400 indictments for "unlawful cohabitation," with an uptick from 1884 to 1886. More than a thousand men were convicted.

Faced with increasingly vigorous federal prosecution, Mormons dealt with these challenges in different ways. Some Mormon leaders took flight, for instance, going on extended missions. Some wives and their children went into hiding. For instance, Martha Hughes Cannon, doctor and plural wife, took her children to Europe for several years to avoid testifying about babies born to polygamous parents and to her own husband's plural marriages. Some who were brought to trial claimed "forgetfulness," not remembering, for example, whether they had been at a wedding in the last month. Others were more forceful; Sarah Nelson, for

7. This 1880s photo from Utah Territory captured the carceral experience of the polygamous husbands known as "cohabs," as they were usually prosecuted for illegal cohabitation with multiple women. During the vigorous federal campaigns against polygamy in the 1880s, many such cohabs went to prison.

instance, beat two deputies with a broomstick when they arrived to arrest her husband's other wives. Apostle Lorenzo Snow hid for a while in a bunker under his living room, but he was found and arrested in late 1885.

Also arrested and then convicted was a major LDS leader and member of the First Presidency, George Q. Cannon, who had previously represented Utah Territory in Congress. It was a mark of his prestige, even among non-Mormons, that when he entered the federal penitentiary in Salt Lake City, the other prisoners did not chant "fresh fish," as they usually did with new arrivals. The federal prison housed Mormon polygamists as well as men convicted of murder and rape; it was a strange mix. Cannon reported that the language with which the non-Mormons profaned God was horrible for the faithful. Still, Cannon enjoyed special privileges, including more space, a mattress, butter for his bread, and regular visits and gifts. Cannon's special perks came, somewhat ironically, from the warden of the penitentiary, who already knew him.

That warden, Arthur Pratt, was none other than the son of Sarah and Orson Pratt, the Quorum member who made the public pronouncement about LDS plural marriage in 1852. Sarah had been Orson's first wife, and she had accommodated further wives as well as years of separation from Orson, who was often away on church business. As Arthur later recalled, Sarah stayed with Orson out of piety and marital duty. In 1868, the situation deteriorated because Sarah was disgusted that Orson, at fifty-seven, started courting a sixteen-year-old as a potential new wife. Then he announced he was going to spend equal time with his wives, so Sarah would see him only one week out of every six. She renounced Mormonism, was excommunicated, and later denounced polygamy publicly. So did her son, Arthur, also excommunicated, who became an antipolygamy crusader. Yet he treated Cannon with respect, even allowing him to lead Sunday school for his fellow LDS prisoners.

Despite the relatively gentle treatment of men like Cannon, this situation was becoming increasingly untenable for the Mormons, especially as more men went to prison and their families were left in disarray, both domestic and financial. In 1890, two further court decisions made the church position even more challenging. One Idaho ruling disfranchised not just actual polygamists, but also anyone who advocated its acceptability. Another decision, *Late Corporation of the Church of Jesus Christ of Latter-day Saints v. United States*, upheld the seizure of church (as well as personal) property of polygamists, thus endangering the financial viability of the church.

In desperation, in 1890, Church President Wilford Woodruff issued a "manifesto" formally agreeing to follow federal law in marriage. He enjoined Mormons not to contract any new marriages that were illegal in the United States. Nevertheless, he made no mention of what was to happen to current plural marriages or to the children of such unions. This official renunciation helped Utah finally achieve statehood in 1896. Still, a number of Mormons disagreed with ending plural marriage, and some continued to practice it regardless. In 1896, Martha Hughes Cannon told a San Francisco newspaper, "I believe in polygamy.... Of course the law of the United States says 'No,' and we must obey. But that does not alter one's belief in the right of the thing." Indeed, through the 1890s, more than half of the Quorum of the Twelve and the First Presidency were involved in polygamy, as were plenty of other Mormons. So, controversies over plural marriages, in Utah and beyond, continued.

Chapter 6
Modern encounters

"We are assumed to live in a group of numerous rivaling wives, and they expect every Turkish man to have a harem of his own, that is, to have at least eight or ten wives," complained one Ottoman princess, Seniha Sultan, in 1910. A privileged woman, she considered these assumptions demeaning and laughable. Such stereotypes nevertheless continued to influence the history of polygamy, which remained a flashpoint for debates in the twentieth and twenty-first centuries.

By 1910, people around the world, including Ottoman princesses, routinely acknowledged that polygamy was considered an outmoded practice, to be rejected by modern people. Those who castigated polygamy thus proved themselves to be enlightened. Monogamy meant shiny and modern progress, while polygamy meant dark and primitive, a "relic of barbarism," as American Republicans had framed it in 1856. An emphasis on monogamy became a mark of national, as well as personal, civility. A feminist critique of the subordination of wives was increasingly part of this trajectory. Some reformers used criticisms of polygamy as ways to assert their superiority over those whom they saw as less progressive members of their own societies, again marking inclusion and exclusion. Moreover, it was a way for imperialists of various stripes to show off their greater advancement over whole nations.

Despite this disapproval, polygamy continued around the world into the twentieth century, although in increasingly altered contexts. The global criticism of polygamy made some people who still practiced it go underground, continuing polygamy but often in more illicit and troubling ways. This situation made polygamy not just seemingly backward but also sometimes criminal. Yet some polygamists refused to accept that it was an inferior form, occasionally even publicizing their plural marriages in media-friendly ways. Some embraced it as a point of distinction from, even defiance against, Western norms. Yet they did so in a context in which polygamy around the world seemed to a lot of people, even in cultures of traditional polygamy, to be inferior, even embarrassing.

The harem had long symbolized despotism and dissipation among Europeans and Americans. Mary Wollstonecraft, in her *Vindication of the Rights of Woman* (1792), argued for women's education on the basis that uneducated women were "weak beings…only fit for a seraglio," unable to raise their children properly. For British feminist campaigners in the nineteenth century, distinguishing orderly monogamy and the relative freedom of its women from the sequestered and constrained lives of women in polygamy elsewhere in the world functioned to underline Western civility. Such claims, too, could be a way to advocate for further freedoms. Suffragists and those seeking to reform married women's property laws contended that British women deserved these changes in law in order to amplify the distance between British women and degraded, victimized plural wives. British publications such as *Thirty Years in the Harem* (1872) by Melek-Hanum, wife of H. H. Kibrizli-Mehemet-Pasha, reinforced such views. A Turkish convert from Islam to Christianity who had resettled in England, she recounted her experiences in repressive polygamy as well as her escape from it. She lamented that secondary, lower-ranking wives who joined the harem were forced to endure "the desires of their master and the terrible jealousy of their mistress." Such attacks on polygyny, from a plural wife, were powerful.

British imperialists in places such as Egypt criticized such harems as well. There, British officials asserted that plural marriages underpinned Egyptian political inferiority. One British visitor explicitly connected Egyptian family practices with its subordination: "Every harem is a little despotism.... If polygamy degrades the wife, deprives the children, and turns the husband into a tyrant, does not that mean that institution alone accounts for Musulman [i.e. Muslim] inferiority?" In the 1890s, the British consul general, Lord Cromer, conceded that Egyptians had made considerable material progress, but "whether any moral progress is possible in a country where polygamy and the absence of family life blights the whole social system is another question." In his view, European superiority rested on its domestic organization. For Lord Cromer, "monogamy fosters family life, polygamy destroys it."

As it happens, Egyptians had already been moving away from polygamy. They sought to distinguish themselves from Europeans and Ottomans in their marriages as in other areas. Increasingly, wealthy urban populations tended to favor smaller family units, monogamous and nuclear. The monarch, Tawfiq, who ruled from 1879 to 1892, distinguished himself from his father and forebears by remaining monogamous. So, in a sense, the direction of travel was already toward monogamy. Outside criticisms merely accelerated trends already present. Still, though there was less polygamy by the turn of the twentieth century, it did not disappear. In fact, Tawfiq's son, Abbas II, took a second wife, though he did so clandestinely, unlike his publicly polygamous grandfather. Monogamy was not seen as entirely antithetical to polygamy; rather, a range of options existed that were suitable for particular circumstances.

By this stage, the chorus of criticisms of polygamy was already growing in Egypt and elsewhere in the Middle East. Educated women condemned polygamy in print; one teacher, Malak Hifni Nasif, decried it in the newspaper as "the fiercest enemy of women." In their memoirs, numerous early twentieth-century Egyptian women recounted unhappiness with plural marriages. The modernizing judge and philosopher, Qasim Amin, took up these issues in his noted publications, *The Liberation of Women* (1899) and *The New Woman* (1901). Amin asserted that monogamy was generally preferable for progressive Egyptian men. As female authors had, Amin pointed out that polygamy, and by extension broader restrictions on women, were not intrinsic to Islam but had been adopted from local cultures prevalent in the past. He noted that under *shari'a*, women had more rights in law to property ownership and distribution than their Western counterparts. He conceded that Islamic law favored men in one area only: polygamy. Yet he posited that while the Qu'ran allowed it, it suggested that restrictions were necessary. For Amin, polygamy bred conflict among wives and among their children. In his view, monogamy was the better choice for men: "a mature, well-bred man, knowledgeable about justice and law, will reject the burden of responsibility placed on his shoulders by marriage to two wives." While he admitted that it might be necessary in cases where a first wife was unable to have either sex or children, he thought that in general it was a relic of the past, incompatible with modern enlightened Muslim masculinity. He concluded, "It is appropriate that men today discard the tradition of polygamy," largely so that men would be more progressive and happier, fitter citizens for a new nation.

Amin and others sang the praises of monogamy, but less for women's happiness than for men's. They sought to demonstrate to Europeans that they were as civilized and worthy of self-rule. Rejecting polygamy proved their credentials as progressive global citizens as well as benign and affectionate husbands and fathers; they were not ignorant peasants trapped in old customs. Modern political reform depended on companionate marriage, monogamous households, and capitalist economies. One Ottoman scholar, Mansurizade Mehmed Sa'id, similarly pushed for change in a series of early twentieth-century newspaper articles, contending Europeans "imagine that medieval savagery still prevails in the Islamic world." Like Amin, he implored Ottoman men as modern Muslims to give up plural marriages. Another Ottoman reformer, Şemseddin Sami, agreed that polygamy was not intrinsic to Islam and that it could rightly be restricted. He thought it appropriate only in cases where the first wife could not have children and where she gave her formal agreement.

Such criticisms of polygamy reflected broader changes in women's roles in Islamic nations. One Ottoman intellectual woman, Fatma Aliye, asserted that the Qu'ran implied that monogamy was a better option for most people and that Islam was eminently compatible with women's rights and progress. As one woman in Istanbul phrased it in 1914 in a religious magazine, "It is not like women's lives have not been affected by the rather significant revolutions taking place in the world of men." This anonymous woman pushed the idea of women's greater participation: "Certain measures may be taken to allow us women to mingle in life." Even some women of the harem went out for public visits and excursions.

In countries keen to show their progress, such as Turkey and Tunisia, leaders used the abolition of polygamy as a quick and relatively easy way to prove their progressive credentials. A 1923 Turkish law that allowed polygamy nevertheless included a significant rider: that the Qu'ran did not require its practice. With the adoption of the Turkish Civil Code in 1926, polygamy was abolished altogether. Tunisia, too, outlawed it, on the basis that it was impossible in practice to treat all cowives with total equity. In fact, by this time, polygamy was quite a restricted practice in Tunisia, as large rural families gave way to smaller urban spaces and families. Outlawing it provoked little by way of popular outcry. Moreover, it had come to be associated with older ruling dynasties, so that its curtailment was a political act aimed at creating more modern governments and structures.

8. Veiled women of the sultan's household go out on a weekend outing, shortly before the Ottoman sultanate ended in 1922.

Polygamy took novel forms elsewhere in Africa, too. There had likely been a harem in the royal court of Benin in southwest Nigeria since the thirteenth century. Despite the global criticisms of polygamy, this harem has continued to be a focal point of political power into the twentieth and even twenty-first centuries. Yet there have been changes in methods, scope, and reactions. Oba Akenzua II, who ruled from 1933 to 1978, allowed reporters into the palace to show off his domestic life, his multiple wives, and children. One of his wives, Ohan Akenzua, accompanied him on a royal visit to England in the 1950s to meet Queen Elizabeth II. Royal wives such as Ohan Akenzua demonstrated their political and diplomatic importance, on both international and national stages. The Benin royal harem itself remains an important political space, where women's groups and individuals have been able to discuss issues and to petition royal wives for political action. Even in the early twenty-first century, these activities augment the authority of the wives and, by extension, the royal family more generally. They support the prominence of the Eson, the Oba's senior wife, who is the leader of the wives (though not necessarily the first wife). In addition, the mother of the king has a political role at court.

Polygamous political systems in Benin have bolstered female authority and political power, but they have had constraining effects, too. For more junior wives, it has been difficult to navigate this harem, and the authority of younger wives has been quite limited. Most young women have viewed becoming a member of the royal harem with considerable trepidation, and often it has been the choice of their family, not the women themselves. Entering the harem has usually meant separation from their own family, and their adultery could result in a death sentence. Since the Oba was the only man who could enter the harem, and he might or might not have sustained relationships with all his wives, there was significant potential for a difficult and lonely existence. The wives usually had financial stability and property, but these, too, could vary depending on their background. Some wives—generally more senior ones from higher-ranking families who had many children—flourished, but other wives—lacking seniority, rank, and/or fertility— did not.

At the same time, for most nonroyal Nigerians, polygamy has endured, but often not in ways fully recognized by law, which has privileged monogamy. Sometimes a man has had a legal, or "inside wife," as well as one or more informal "outside wives." The outside wives, lacking formal status, have enjoyed little in the way of legal protection. This situation can be difficult for all the wives. This lack of formal recognition for polygamy can make it even more challenging for the outside wives, as they often have had little legal recognition in situations of abuse or unhappiness. They have also often lacked financial resources and so have had to remain in situations that they might otherwise choose to leave. Again, poorer women fare worse.

Similar dynamics characterize polygamy in other modern global contexts as well. In Siam, polygamy had flourished among the royal household and the well-off more generally over centuries, shoring up the power of the monarch and those loyal to him. In the eighteenth and nineteenth centuries, outsiders attacked this system, seeing it as a backward, perverse practice harmful to women. Such claims did potent political work internationally, putting Siam's place as a "civilized nation" in jeopardy. One of the most well-known accounts of Siamese polygamy came from the pen of an Anglo-Indian woman, Anna Leonowens, who worked as an English teacher and governess at the royal court. Her account became famous and served as the basis for the musical *The King and I*. Leonowens published multiple accounts of her life in the court of Siam, tapping into Western appetites for the exotic, erotic East. She penned highly successful accounts of her time in the "harem" after she had spent time in the United States, where she imbibed the political connections between polygamy and slavery drawn by anti-Mormon crusades. She acknowledged that "every harem is a little world in itself, composed entirely of women,— some who rule, others who obey, and those who serve." Yet overall she found the institution oppressive. Celebrating the bravery and heroism of what she dismissed as "poor, doomed women," Leonowens related lurid tales of the suffering of beautiful, red-lipped young women held in the harem, in chains, "naked to the waist," trapped as a result of the "barbarous cruelty of the palace life."

Still, despite these sensationalist denunciations for Western audiences, Thai polygamy continued. Yet it took new forms in ways unappreciated and unmentioned by people like Leonowens. Debates about it occurred amid shifting political landscapes. It has puzzled historians that despite a move to end it in the mid-nineteenth century, polygamy continued to be legal until it was finally abolished in 1935, little short of six hundred years after it had been enshrined in Siamese law. Some traditionalists, like King Chulalongkorn, or Rama V, continued to practice and in fact expand polygamy, with more than three thousand women resident in the Inner Palace at his death in 1910. Along with Rama V, others supported its continued practice, asserting that Buddhism was compatible with a Siamese modernity that included polygamy.

By contrast, other monarchs, such as Rama V's son, later to become King Vajiravudh, or Rama VI, insisted that polygamy should be ended, deploying accusations of domestic "debauchery" against rivals who continued to practice it. Rama VI publicly castigated middle-class men who dared to keep "secret wives." As it happened, such men tended to be those who advocated for limits on the monarchy, pushing for more representative forms of government and greater freedoms. King Rama VI, rejecting polygamy, could disparage such "modernizing" men for their sexual excesses and hypocritical domestic practices in keeping plural wives. In this way, Rama VI and others associated political radicalism with sexual immorality, claiming the moral high ground of monogamy. If Thai men did not see eye to eye on polygamy, neither did women. Some defended the older ways, others found themselves in the new situation of middle-class polygamy, and still others condemned the institution. Overall, though, even newer types of polygamy in the modern era rarely worked to empower women.

Even modern polyandry did not necessarily empower wives, as in rural China, one of the rare global examples of women with multiple husbands. This practice arose in the Qing era, from the seventeenth to the early twentieth centuries, as the number of landless and luckless rural poor rose. What was called "getting a husband to support a husband" was a form of nonfraternal polyandry in which a wife, often one whose first husband was ill or injured or otherwise unable to maintain a household, took a male lover who provided financial backing to the family. Some of these arrangements were formal marriages, with contracts. Legal texts from various regions in China reproduced contracts for formal polyandry.

In one 1869 polyandry case reprinted in *The Private Law of Taiwan*, Wang Yunfa, married to Li Xiuliang, fell ill and became paralyzed; he could produce neither income nor heirs. This family consulted a matchmaker and formally arranged for a man named Wu Jinwen to become Li's second husband. Any children born were to be heirs to both the Wu and the Wang families. Formal contracts suggest the permanence of some of these arrangements, which could last for decades. Sometimes, in probably a third of cases, wives themselves instigated these relationships, taking up with another man to help the family financially. At the other end of the spectrum, these could essentially form systems in which the husband pimped out his wife to other men on a very short-term basis. Still, they usually required some degree of cooperation on the part of the wives, at least to succeed and function in a long-term way. They were never considered an ideal solution, and participants often suffered some degree of stigma. They stemmed from bleak rural poverty, a skewed sex ratio (and lack of potential wives), and a thriving market for women and their productive, sexual, and reproductive labor (so that they became concubines or maids of wealthier men, thus leaving fewer wives for poorer men). Informal polygyny of the elite partly drove this polyandry among the poor, a strategy resting on the willingness and work of wives, to keep the family together in difficult circumstances.

American Mormon wives and husbands, too, worked to keep families together after the formal ending of polygamy in 1890. Even after the LDS Church formally advised its members to avoid contracting plural marriage that year, numerous Mormons refused to do so; others remained in existing plural marriages. There were conflicts at the highest levels of the LDS Church. Some of those who believed in the Principle would not accept the Woodruff Manifesto, which had called for an end to new plural marriages. Some of these individuals took refuge in less populated areas in Utah and Arizona. Others escaped to colonies established in the 1880s in Mexico, such as Colonia Juárez. In such locations, some Mormons continued to live the Principle as they had previously done. One second wife, Mary Eliza Tracy Allred, recorded a memoir in the 1930s, recalling with pleasure her admiration for the first wife, Phoebe, a "lovely" woman. The Allreds fled to Mexico and lived together in a modest house, humbly but apparently happily. Mary Allred noted that for twenty-five years, "we loved each other more devotedly at the end of our companionship than at the beginning." Yet this relocation was in fact a dislocation for many Mormons. Some husbands even attempted to skirt the law by settling one wife and family in Mexico while keeping another family in Utah.

Other Mormon plural spouses went north to Canada, under the leadership of Charles Ora Card, who founded the town of Cardston. In 1886, he had been arrested for polygamy in Utah; he had four wives. Before he could be tried, though, he absconded and moved with his family to the area north of Alberta, Canada. They settled on land near the Kanai (Blood) Reserve, in part for economic reasons but also because they had plans for missionary activity among the local First Nations people. His third wife was Zina Young Card, a daughter of Brigham Young. Like her husband, she was an enthusiastic supporter of polygamy, declaring how happy her childhood in the large, bustling, and decidedly polygamous Young household had been. In fact, one visitor to this region noted with some surprise that "the Mormon women-folk [were] the strongest supporters of polygamy."

Charles Card and two other leaders sought to gain formal permission from the Canadian government to continue their religious practices, including polygamy. They traveled to Ottawa to meet with the prime minister, John A. Macdonald. They subsequently wrote to him to ask that, as they had been previously "subjected to sore persecution" by the US government for their polygamy, they be allowed to live with their families. They wanted to avoid having to cast off their "tender and devoted" wives to "a cold world…[requesting]…an asylum in the Dominion of

Canada." They pointedly reminded Macdonald that they brought wealth, experience, and new young settlers to this country.

Canadians were welcoming, but only to a point. They were no more prepared to countenance polygamy than US authorities had been. Macdonald permitted the Mormons to settle in Canada, but he nevertheless warned them that polygamy was illegal and unacceptable. Macdonald even declared in the House of Commons that "whether [immigrants] are Mohammedans or Mormons, when they come here they must obey the laws of Canada." Yet again there was the specter of Islamic forms of polygamy, with their presumed despotism and lawlessness. Other members of Parliament, worried by the arrival of these renegades, slammed polygamy as an "abomination," "a serious moral and national ulcer." Such views peppered Canadian newspapers, with the *Edmonton Bulletin* announcing in 1887 that "no country, much less a young and sparsely peopled country, can afford to allow ... social abominations to spread merely because the iniquities are performed under the name of religion." The *Edmonton Bulletin* questioned the logic of encouraging the Mormons, who seemed to them much like "the Mohometans of Soudan" or the "Thugs of India," again violent tyrants in popular imaginings.

Such statements linked monogamy with Canadian national strength and polygamy with problematic Asian practices. Even a Canadian advice manual of the era castigated polygamy as a degenerate practice, weakening fertility and strength so that "the Mormons of Utah would soon sink into a state of Asiatic effeminacy." As it happens, Mormons arrived at the same time as other immigrants who also worried Canadian authorities with their domestic practice: the Chinese. An 1885 Royal Commission on Chinese Immigration included one witness who asserted, "They are not the same as we are. They do not respect the Sabbath or wives. Their wives here ... are their second wives, and chiefly prostitutes." One minister, R. C. Houghton, railed against polygamy as an institution "subversive of God's order … its blighting influences are felt and seen in every department of national life" in Asian countries.

Concerns about the polygamy of the newest arrivals to Canada merged with long-standing concerns about that of its oldest inhabitants: the indigenous people who had lived there for centuries before the arrival of Europeans. Plural marriage was a known practice among most First Nations people as well as among some métis people. What Europeans castigated as "polygamy" did not even have an equivalent in the Cree or Blackfoot languages, suggesting that it was simply seen as marriage, a variation of a known and unobjectionable form of domestic organization. As elsewhere, higher-ranking families most commonly practiced it, and it was generally limited in scope. Usually, a man consulted with the first wife before taking additional wives. Presiding over a polygamous household as a senior wife tended to enhance the status of the first wife and the household, since it added labor and children. In fact, occasionally, it was the first wife herself who proposed a sister or another woman as a secondary wife. Widows sometimes joined a household as secondary wives, supporting a larger family or kin network.

There were good reasons for some First Nations women, and men, to enter into plural marriage. First, there was sometimes a serious demographic imbalance because of war. For instance, an 1806 census by the North West Company found that there were just over 7,500 native men but more than 17,000 women. Polygamy in such conditions could make a great deal of sense. Wives in polygamy tended to have fewer children, thus easing their burden in terms of pregnancies, nursing, and childcare. At the same time, women performed much critical household labor, here as in other times and places, and so sometimes wives themselves wanted help and companionship. A woman might even marry into a polygamous household knowing that she would be joining a sort of domestic team, instead of going it alone.

9. This drawing by a European observer shows a métis, or mixed-race, man in Canada with his two First Nations wives. They all wear a mix of Amerindian and European items, and the wife on the left carries a baby on her back.

In First Nations plural marriages, wives divided labor, thus allowing for greater specialization and shared burdens. One Blackfoot woman, Middle Woman No Coat, recalled in a 1939 interview that in her childhood household, two older wives did the tanning of hides while the younger wives did the cooking. All the wives took turns collecting firewood and tending the household fire in winter. One Dakota man in the 1950s recounted that his father had had two wives who shared the quill and ribbon work and who continued to live and labor together even after their husband had died. Wives took care of each other's children as well. Annie Sioux of the Dakota recalled that one wife stayed home with the children while the other wife went on errands into town. She thought it worked well. Maxidiwiac, or Buffalo Bird Woman, of the Hidatsa remembered that her own mother and another wife had died when she was six, but two other wives, whom she also called mothers, raised her and her siblings, with no distinction made between children of different wives.

Of course, even in relatively harmonious situations, there were occasional tensions and hierarchies between wives. A twentieth-century Kainai historian, Beverly Hungry Wolf, reported older stories in which "a man had two wives, one of whom was his favorite and the other of whom had to do all the work and was generally mistreated." Although a Cree chief, Fine Day, recalled that his mother, a second wife, and the first wife had gotten along well, "the first wife was always the boss." One Sikisa wife could not have children. She persuaded her husband eventually to take first one of her sisters, and then two more of them, as additional wives. She became a mother to all of her nieces and nephews, and it was a relatively happy household. However, the first wife always retained a position of importance, what the Blackfoot called the "sits-beside-him" wife. This first wife was the co-head of the household and its manager. She accompanied her husband to feasts and ceremonies, with high visibility and standing in the community. The other wives did not have such a privileged role, though they had fewer public obligations.

Despite long-standing and reasonably tranquil practices of plural marriage in the country, Canadian authorities still denounced these practices, casting them into the usual mold of problematic and backward. Missionaries, as ever, led the charge against polygamy. One sympathetic fur trader, himself with two wives, noted, "The first thing a missionary does is abuse the Indian for having a plurality of wives." One Blackfoot leader warned the missionaries off this topic, informing them that he himself had eight wives whom he loved and with whom he had children. He demanded, "Which am I to keep and which put away?'" Such was not an easy question for missionaries, but they continued to preach Christian monogamy. Secular authorities, too, deemed native marriage an inferior form. One 1867 court case, *Connolly v. Woolrich and Johnson et al.*, described Cree people as "barbarians" with only "infidel laws." The court ruled that since even monogamous Cree marriages were potentially polygamous, they were always primitive and inferior to Christian marriage. Some legal decisions went even further, as in the 1884 Quebec case of *Fraser v. Pouliot*, in which all native marriages were derided simply as "concubinage" or mere "relations of male and female in savage life."

Despite such dismissals of indigenous marriages, there was little appetite for prosecuting polygamy—at least until the arrival of the Mormons in the 1880s and 1890s. At that point, the government became more concerned about these practices and worked to end them. In part, the settlement of Mormons at Cardston, near Blackfoot lands, worried authorities. The Blackfoot did trade with Charles Card, whom even they called "Many Wives." The Department of Indian Affairs began to attempt to eradicate polygamy, stepping up their denunciations and even withholding allowances. Still, their actions remained hesitant and not especially effective. Chief Red Crow of the Kainai continued to live with his four wives, despite government efforts and even his own baptism as a Roman Catholic in 1896.

Efforts to end polygamy among Native Americans in the United States fared little better. In 1895, the US government tried to use the Edmunds Act of 1882, which outlawed polygamy in federal territories, to prosecute American Horse, an indigenous leader with four wives. According to the *Rapid City Daily Journal*, the United States was trying "to make an example" of him to "break up the practice of polygamy among the Indians.'" Authorities arrested American Horse and other leaders. The cases did not succeed, though, as the men claimed, successfully, that their arrests violated treaty provisions that protected "ancient rights and customs." The US government conceded this point, allowing that the Edmunds Act applied only to Mormons and not to Indians. Yet indigenous plural marriage continued to vex authorities in the United States, as in Canada.

Indigenous plural marriages concerned missionaries and authorities in other anglophone imperial spaces as well. In both Australia and New Zealand, colonial authorities attempted to curtail native polygamy. Australian missionaries such as Ernest Gribble, working in Yarrabah in the Queensland region, used every method he could to end polygamy among the Gunggandji and other native groups with whom he lived. He tried to persuade leaders such as Menmuny, who had six wives, to give up plural marriage. Although two wives did leave and remarry, this likely had little to do with Gribble's efforts. Gribble offered "white weddings" with large feasts to those willing to marry in church. One of Menmuny's wives, Nora, did finally agree to such a church wedding, though she insisted on wearing red, not white. Others seemingly accepted all the trappings of the white wedding, including a lavish feast for numerous guests, but without necessarily committing to monogamy. When such enticements did not work, Gribble punished polygamists and others; he resorted to caning, locking people up in chains, and denying them food. Despite his much-vaunted moral superiority in domestic matters, Gribble himself had an unhappy marriage with a woman named Emilie and pursued a long-term relationship with an Aboriginal woman named Jeannie. It was not polygamy, but neither was it Christian monogamy. It is little wonder that his efforts were not especially successful.

Even though there were thus gray areas, the dangerous possibilities of colonial contact led many colonial authorities to underscore the distinctions to be drawn between primitive polygamy and modern monogamy. In the first decades of British colonization in New Zealand, imperial law allowed the continuation of customary practices of Māori marriages, including polygamy. This situation changed in the later nineteenth century, especially with legal decisions such as that of *Wi Parata v. The Bishop of Wellington* in 1877. In this case, the chief justice of the New Zealand Supreme Court, Sir James Prendergast, declared that prior to British conquest, New Zealand was "thinly peopled by barbarians without any form of law or civil government." By this logic, there was no need to continue to honor any treaties or to respect domestic practices, including plural marriage, among Māori people. In the 1909 case, *Rex v. Kingi*, the court maintained, "If the Māori people were permitted to go back to Māori custom with respect to marriages, and to call those unions marriages, that might include polygamous marriages...the Court does not recognise the so-called marriages." Here, as in Canada, any indigenous marriage, potentially polygamous, was considered an inferior and barbaric union, not a true marriage recognized by law. Such views were echoed in newspapers; an article in the *Otago Daily Times* in 1897, for instance, condemned polygamy as an inferior form of union. Such articles, as well as legal decisions, helped to cast Māori plural marriages as unacceptable under New Zealand law. In part, the refusal of a number of legal regimes to recognize polygamy often worked to disempower the very plural wives and children whom antipolygamy regulations were meant to protect. Such dynamics continue to underlie polygamy globally into the twenty-first century.

Chapter 7
Contemporary debates

Dynamite, the law, and continued efforts at eradication have not blasted polygamy out of the contemporary world. In July 1953, the state governments of Arizona and Utah launched a secret raid on a border community in Short Creek, Arizona. They knew that there was a growing and, in their view, pernicious presence there, and they wanted to cut its practices off at the knees. They arrived at four in the morning, announcing their presence by sending a stick of dynamite sailing through the summer sky above the sleepy town. Authorities then headed into the houses of the local inhabitants with warrants for no fewer than 122 arrests. The crimes included cohabitation, bigamy, rape, and statutory rape. Trials took place over months and even years, and they involved some of the most powerful polygamous families living in Short Creek. Ultimately, though, these efforts and later raids did not have the effect authorities had hoped.

Polygamy has neither withered away nor disappeared by force in the twenty-first century. Instead, it has taken on novel forms in altered contexts, some of which are especially troubling for women and children. There has been a resurgence of polygamy in a number of countries since that 1953 raid. Countries in the Middle East (such as Saudi Arabia), Asia (such as Malaysia), and Africa (such as South Africa) have seen continued controversies over plural marriage. Polygamy remains illegal in a lot of places, including most of the fifty United States and Canada. Periodically, governments take aim at this practice and attempt to end it. Yet numerous families around the world have continued to practice this form of marriage.

In some contexts, this revival of polygamy has been connected with religious fundamentalism and limits on women's public participation. In these new contexts, protective features of traditional polygamy have eroded, so that the newer forms of polygamy are actually more conservative and oppressive than the older, "traditional" forms they purportedly replicate. Sometimes, too, the continued illicit nature of polygamy means that it has gone underground, making it that much harder for government and society to regulate it. In seeking to protect women and children from polygamy by making it illegal, authorities may have inadvertently and ironically further endangered women and children. The continued stigma against it has carried unfortunate consequences for those living it.

Along with this conservative resurgence of polygamy, there has been pressure on monogamy from left-wing critics, who question married monogamy as the correct or only path for domestic organization. They highlight forms of sexuality and affection beyond one plus one. There is a liberal, even libertarian, celebration of "poly," especially polyamory in Western liberal democracies: not polygamy and certainly not traditional, but not unrelated. With the agitation for same-sex marriage as a legal right around the world, feminist and queer scholars, as well as advocates for polyamory and what is termed ethical nonmonogamy, have suggested that there might be versions of modern polygamy that are neutral or even positive for women and families. Some contemporary representations of polygamy, including popular television shows, have given Americans in particular a more sympathetic vision of even "fundamentalist Mormon" polygamy. The notion that there might be pleasant polygamists next door may yet alter the dynamics of antipolygamy—and polygamy. Increasingly conservative and repressive forms of polygamy exist, along with feminist and queer critiques of monogamy and sympathy for polygamists. Both reflect pressures and changes of the contemporary era, albeit in very different ways. So, as ever, polygamy takes new shapes in novel times, despite much continuity in condemnations of it.

Polygamy in some Islamic countries has become a potent political choice. Given the antipolygamy hostility of nations in Europe and the Americas, to permit and practice it has become a form of resistance to Western values and impositions, even an anticolonial measure. In such situations, to denounce critics of polygamy, including feminists—cast as complicit with Western hegemony— becomes an act of piety. Yet the versions often practiced in the contemporary era in fact depart in significant ways from those practiced in earlier eras. The invented tradition of much contemporary Islamic polygamy is exactly that, and the versions of it in common use seem less protective of women than previous ones. There has been an uptick in the practice of polygamy in several Islamic nations, including Saudi Arabia, Iran, Egypt, Jordan, and Sudan. It has supporters in Mauritania, Algeria, Uganda, and Turkey, too (though it is not legal there). Sometimes there is rivalry between countries, with each vying to outdo the other in its support for polygamy, as a form of salafism, or emulation of *salaf al-salih*, the pure forebears of early Islam. Thus Iran, a Shi'ite majority country, seeks to position itself as the voice of "true Islam" with vigorous support for polygamy and the veiling of women. Moreover, they point to the long-standing Shi'ite endorsement of *mut'ah*, or temporary, marriages, the very issue that vexed Akbar and his scholars in the Mughal Empire. Saudi Arabia, which is predominantly Sunni, equally loudly voices its support for polygamy and veiling, thus maintaining that it, not Iran, represents "true Islam."

Yet polygamy is a source of considerable internal debate in Saudi Arabia, a nation unusual in its oil riches and its social customs.

Some Saudis uphold monogamy and companionate marriages, while others claim the tradition of polygamy as a marker of holiness, again linked with salafism. Several Saudi religious leaders promote polygamy. Their writings tend to condemn wives who prefer monogamy as selfishly preventing their husbands from helping to support other women, including single and widowed ones. A 2001 *fatwa* issued by the Grand *Mufti* of Saudi Arabia called for women to accept polygamy as a key aspect of the Islamic faith. Saudi authorities assure women that good Islamic wives accept polygamy without hesitation. They aver that its use prevents sexually transmitted diseases and immorality by channeling men's sexual energies into wives, instead of lovers. Conservative leaders praise polygamy for rendering even "mannish, masculine women of the feminist movement" more docile, feminine, and pious.

Saudi polygamy has taken on novel forms. Rising in popularity, it has spread to new kinds of practitioners, as an educated urban elite has increasingly adopted it, a result both of these Islamic teachings and of the great riches from oil that enable more husbands to afford it. Yet its traditional rural practice came out of a context in which oversight by an extended family helped to ensure that the husband maintained equality between wives and in which a larger network of kin helped wives and their children to navigate it. Since a number of the urban, educated families who have started practicing polygamy more recently have been more nuclear in style, these older networks of support—financial, practical, and emotional—are no longer intact. This situation can lead to isolation. At the same time, there remains some disapproval of it and a sense that second wives and their children in particular are less significant to the larger family.

There are some positive stories, but the tensions of the system are evident. Some wives, first and second, appreciate the greater amount of independence polygamy can bring. One observer spoke with a pair of cowives who took care of each other's children on the nights the other wife was with the husband, and all the children behaved as if they belonged to both women. Yet the realities of polygamy are more complicated than its proponents may publicly allow. Women who were interviewed related that there could be resentments and jealousies. Numerous Saudi first wives who entered into what they presumed would be monogamous marriages have found the transition to polygamy rocky, as did Mormon first wives such as Emma Smith. One Saudi first wife complained that although she was proud that her husband preferred her cooking and organizational talents to those of his second wife, "even these skills now work against me; he calls as [he and the other wife] are both planning a day together by the seaside and says he will... [come by only to]... pick up his favourite packed lunch." Second wives, too, endure jealousies and public disapproval. Children of polygamy worry over the absences of their father when the mothers live apart, and the stresses on mothers affect them, too.

Some of these concerns about the practice of polygamy appear among Muslims in other countries as well. In Morocco, Syria, Iraq, and Pakistan, laws require that first wives and/or the court grant permission to husbands to take additional wives. There are similar controls in place in Malaysia. Yet there is not always strict adherence to these policies. The Malaysian Islamic Family Law Act of 1984 permitted polygamy while at the same time setting a range of constraints on its practice. A married man who wanted to marry another woman had to apply to the court, proving that this second marriage was just and necessary, with wives and children all financially supported and treated equally. He also had to prove that the first wife would not be harmed or financially disadvantaged. Yet many men failed to observe these stipulations. In 2003, a group called Sisters in Islam organized a "Campaign for Monogamy," advancing a program of stricter oversight and control, on the basis that it was almost impossible to treat all wives equitably. They deployed the theories of an Islamic modernist, Abdullah Yusuf Ali, to press the case for monogamy within Islam. The effort has not always succeeded, but they have tried, in part by stressing that they are not antipolygamy but simply in favor of justice in Islamic marriages.

One of the more well-known examples of contemporary non-Muslim polygamy is that of the South African politician, Jacob Zuma, who served as president of South Africa from 2009 to 2018 as a member of the African National Congress. He married six women, though one left him and one died. He embraced plural marriage as a Zulu custom, and his wives have been well-educated women, pictured with him at public events when he was president. Yet there were reports of Zuma fathering illegitimate children and abusing women sexually, as well as claims of corruption in his government. For most South Africans, his marriages have been among the least troubling aspects of his behavior. Other South Africans, including some women, have championed plural marriages. One South African newspaper in 2017 reported on the advantages of plural marriage for wives, quoting Cultural, Religious and Linguistic Rights Commission chairwoman Thoko Mkhwanazi-Xaluva that "it is more legally and economically empowering to be in a polygamous marriage than to be a mistress." In part, such support for polygamy stems from a sense that it represents an enduring connection with South African indigenous traditions, a way of circumventing European impositions.

Although the LDS Church has renounced polygamy, "fundamentalist Mormons" (disavowed by the mainstream LDS Church) continue to practice it. There are forty thousand to sixty thousand members of such religious groups in the United States, many fewer than the six million or so mainstream Mormons. Certainly, the forms of polygamy practiced by these "fundamentalists" often depart substantially from nineteenth-century practices of Mormon polygamy as well as from contemporary Mormon life. There is considerable variety between these communities, from the Apostolic United Brethren to the

Latter-day Church of Christ, or Kingston Clan, to Fundamentalist Latter-day Saints (FLDS). Still, all agree on the importance of the Principle of plural marriage lived in highly patriarchal and fairly isolated communities, mostly in bastions in the intermountain west of the United States. Rulon Allred founded an Apostolic United Brethren community in Bluffdale, Utah, in the 1950s, after a split with other fundamentalist Mormon leaders in the wake of the Short Creek raids. He had previously been a mainstream Mormon with a single wife, who left him when he decided to pursue polygamy. The Kingston Clan is a highly isolated and secretive community in which population growth by a select few families (the Clan) is considered the ideal, involving both incest and sex with minors, a deeply unsavory and pernicious set of practices.

The FLDS form the largest and most well-known group, with at least ten thousand members. Their epicenter is at the border of Utah and Arizona, in the towns of Hildale, Utah, and Colorado City, Arizona, formerly Short Creek. This area attracted polygamous families beginning in the 1920s as part of a wider exodus of such families. They developed what they saw as continuities with earlier polygamy theology in periodicals such as *Truth Magazine*, founded by Joseph Musser. Musser advised followers that husbands should have no sexual involvement with their wives from the point of conception to the end of weaning. He cautioned them, with advice that echoed Augustine of Hippo, that "a man who looks upon his wife with lust is damned." Despite the relative self-sufficiency and isolation of these communities, they have remained a thorn in the side of authorities in Utah and Arizona. There is constant concern over the possibility of sexual exploitation of young women. Yet most of the prosecutions launched in 1953 fizzled out, and they had little effect on changing behavior in this community.

In fact, after the Short Creek raids, FLDS has only become more patriarchal, isolated, and repressive. From the 1950s to his death in 1986, the FLDS was led by Leroy Johnson, whom members saw as a kindly and avuncular presence, "Uncle Roy." After Johnson's death, Rulon Jeffs took over the group and proceeded to consolidate power in a number of ways. He took the title of "Prophet" (which Johnson had never used), and there was a much greater level of centralized control. He arranged marriages of young women to older men, and he expelled those who disagreed with him. There had previously been alliances with a related group in Bountiful, Canada, led by Winston Blackmore. After criticizing Jeffs, Blackmore was cut off.

When Rulon Jeffs died in 2002, he left twenty-two wives and more than sixty children. One of those children, Warren Jeffs, took over the group as well as the title of Prophet. Jeffs married several of his father's widows, arranging marriages for himself and others with girls under eighteen; he was subsequently convicted of child sex abuse. After fleeing from federal prosecution and spending a year on the Ten Most Wanted list issued by the US Federal Bureau of Investigation, Jeffs was caught and convicted of sexual assault against minors. He remains in prison, serving a life sentence. Since his imprisonment, the FLDS leadership has been in disarray, but a number of the FLDS faithful still consider him the president and Prophet of the FLDS.

The crimes of Warren Jeffs came to national and international attention in part because of another unsuccessful US raid, in 2008, on a new compound, the Yearning for Zion Ranch set up by the FLDS near Eldorado, Texas. Fearing prosecution by Utah authorities, of the kind that had resulted in the Short Creek debacle, the FLDS decided to found their own new self-sufficient community in a remote part of Texas. This ranch was organized under the leadership of Jeffs's ally, Merril Jessop, who was later convicted as an accomplice to rape. In April 2008, phone calls to a family violence hotline reported that there was abuse of minors there. Authorities from the Texas Department of Family and Protective Services raided the ranch and removed more than four

hundred children, thought to be under threat because of activities
of underage sex and assault. More than one hundred mothers
voluntarily accompanied the children into care. The courts in
Texas subsequently ruled that children could not be removed from
their families in this way, although several underage mothers were
identified. Most of the leaders, including Jeffs, were indicted for
crimes such as bigamy, sexual assault, sex with minors, and
trafficking minors across state lines. In 2014, the state of Texas
took over the ranch, and it remains in state possession. Its loss
was a financial blow, and its leaders remain in prison.
Nevertheless, polygamy and a range of related practices still exist
in these communities, so it is not clear whether these raids have
had much effect.

The notorious events in Texas did succeed in making polygamy the
subject of considerable media attention. Although the FLDS had
been functioning for decades, suddenly people around the country
and the world saw American polygamy in vivid and lurid ways,
with ominously patriarchal leaders, seemingly exploited mothers
clad in plain pastel "prairie dresses," with their long hair in
distinctive French braids and their many children. These plural
wives seemed to be under intense and sometimes illicit male
control, and certainly FLDS codes do require wives to be obedient
and subordinate to their husbands. In the public eye, polygamy
became inextricably connected with underage sexual violation and
other repugnant crimes and thus gained a new and more troubling
face. It seemed to confirm the notion that women in such systems
could only ever be dupes and victims of salacious and power-
hungry men who overrode the law to pursue their sordid desires.

A range of books and television shows echoed these enduring
tropes. There are several first-person published accounts of
women who had fled the control of polygamous and tyrannical
husbands and a few of "lost boys"—young men forced out of the
communities so as not to compete with older men for young
wives. Among the most notable memoirs was that by Carolyn

Jessop, one of the plural wives of Merril, the man in charge of setting up the Yearning for Zion Ranch. Her account presents a grim vision of what life in these communities could be like. She was raised in a strictly disciplined FLDS family in isolation from most non-FLDS contact. She was married off at eighteen without much notice to a man she did not know, who, at fifty-four, was older than her father. She was his fourth wife, and he proceeded to take several more. She struggled to find a place in the household when she did not immediately become pregnant. The emphasis on fertility among the FLDS means that wives gain favor by having numerous children, and it can be very challenging for those who do not. The number of children, and the sexual favor of a husband, can increase the status of a wife, and their absence can diminish it. There are hierarchies between wives, as well as husbands. Carolyn Jessop's account is from the perspective of a woman who has escaped and sued her ex-husband for custody, which she won, so it is not obviously positive about life among the FLDS. Yet one of her own daughters returned to the FLDS, so not all women, even those exposed to the outside world, want to escape it.

These American polygamous situations can be extremely problematic, but as in other contexts, some plural wives evidently find peace in their situation. As elsewhere, there are strong female networks, shared childcare, and a sense of driving religious purpose. In one fundamentalist family in Pinesdale, Montana, each of the four wives did different jobs—one was a nurse, two took care of children and home, and a fourth taught school. However, the intense power struggles among the men leading groups such as the FLDS mean that wives and children have become pawns in their conflicts. The position of such wives has deteriorated as these groups have grown even more isolated. Younger men, too, have suffered for being expelled from these communities.

To the intense dismay of the LDS Church, these communities claim continuities with nineteenth-century Mormon theology and the revelation of men like Joseph Smith. There are some basic parallels: men like Brigham Young did marry multiple women as part of their leadership, and a few of the wives were under the age of eighteen. Still, this practice of marrying women under eighteen was more commonly accepted and practiced in the nineteenth century than it is in the early twenty-first century. In addition, such women had straightforward access to divorce and continued contact with their birth families and communities. They participated in public activities, including running relief societies and working on newspapers such as the *Woman's Exponent*, as well as voting and otherwise living much like other American women of their times. They were even occasionally teachers and doctors in the world. They were seen as outliers, but in significant ways their lives looked much like those of other Americans. Even a wife and son of the church father who advocated for polygamy, Orson Pratt, could publicly leave his household, denounce the practice of polygamy, and yet still live cheerfully enough in Utah, surrounded by practicing Mormons. They were not forced to escape at night, as Carolyn Jessop and others have had to do, to gain safety for their children and their selves. The versions of fundamentalist polygamy in the twentieth and twenty-first centuries, then, are far darker and more oppressive to women as well as to both girls and boys.

As in places like Saudi Arabia, this polygamy is an invented tradition departing in vital ways from the actual tradition it purports to uphold, supporting religious repression and an ever smaller and more powerful cabal of male leaders. Those prairie dresses and braids on contemporary fundamentalist plural wives epitomize the crafted nature of these so-called traditions, including polygamy. Most people who see them in press reports imagine them to be simply a throwback to an earlier age. But they are not. They deliberately invoke the nineteenth-century past, but in very particular ways. There are no brightly sprigged calicos, no ruffles, no corseted waists. In the nineteenth century, Mormon plural wives would have been largely indistinguishable from other American wives based on their appearance. Yet these fundamentalist wives bear almost no resemblance to modern young women, even modest Mormon ones. These outfits are plainer and more uniform even than those worn by LDS plural wives of an earlier era. Even plural wives in Short Creek in 1953 look much like other 1950s housewives, so something changed in these communities from 1953 to 2008.

These new forms of American polygamy, driven ever further underground, suggest to many that polygamy should be decriminalized or even legalized so as to prevent the harms now

10. This photo, one of many taken during the raid on Fundamentalist Church of Jesus Christ of Latter-day Saints houses in Short Creek, Arizona in 1953, shows the plural wives and the children of a single household. Unlike later members of this church, this family looks much like similar nonfundamentalist families of their era, with the wives wearing patterned dresses and aprons.

associated with it. Even Carolyn Jessop herself, though strongly opposed to the practices of the polygamous community in which she was raised, has publicly spoken in favor of decriminalization. In her view, the police and the courts mostly turn a blind eye to its practice anyway, so decriminalizing polygamy would mean that those suffering under these regimes would be better able to seek help from the state. According to this contention, decriminalizing polygamy would bring more legal regulation, thus affording greater protections to those living in it. The state of Utah did in fact decriminalize it in 2020. Voices in favor of decriminalization, not enthusiastic about polygamy but willing to tolerate it, appear then to be gaining some traction in the United States.

Despite decriminalization, there has been little push for full legal recognition of polygamy in the United States. In fact, in the early 2000s, as the movement for legalizing same-sex marriage grew, polygamy was frequently invoked as a "slippery slope" argument against same-sex marriage. The claim was that if the United States legalized same-sex marriage, it would alter marriage fundamentally and thus open the door to less acceptable practices such as polygamy. Some justices on the US Supreme Court have made exactly this argument. Justice Antonin Scalia made it in the dissent to a 2003 decision to decriminalize same-sex sex in *Lawrence v. Texas*. In 2015, Chief Justice John Roberts made similar contentions in a dissent to the *Obergefell v. Hodges* decision legalizing same-sex marriage. Roberts noted, "Indeed, from the standpoint of history and tradition, a leap from opposite-sex marriage to same-sex marriage is much greater than one from a two-person union to plural unions, which have deep roots in some cultures around the world. If the majority is willing to take the big leap, it is hard to see how it can say no to the shorter one." Yet, so far, Americans have not taken that short leap. Plural marriages lack legal recognition in any state. There seems to be little prospect of that situation changing anytime soon.

However, American attitudes to polygamy may be softening. Popular representations in American television series have made polygamy seem, if not appealing, at least tolerable. HBO's series *Big Love* (2006–11) was a fictional treatment of what looks like fundamentalist polygamy, with various well-known actors. TLC's *Sister Wives*, a reality series, revolves around the Brown family, with four wives, Meri, Janelle, Christine, and Robyn, their husband Kody, and their eighteen (and counting) children. Both of these popular series have shown polygamy in a more positive light, because both families are essentially suburban, bourgeois, and unthreatening. The shows (especially *Big Love*) hint at salacious aspects, but the families depicted seem much like other middle-class American families, with happy moments (family camping) and some more challenging ones (consulting a marriage therapist). Although evidently espousing some basic theological and social principles at odds with those of many, if not most, Americans, they seem otherwise fairly unobjectionable, even likable. Such representations have likely made polygamy seem less outlandish to Americans, even if they might not choose it for themselves.

Tolerance for nonmonogamy seems to be growing in the United States. A YouGov poll in 2020 suggested ever higher percentages of Americans, perhaps as many as 20 percent, have considered or were living in nonmonogamous relationships. Figures are even higher for Generation Z, born around 2000, with nearly 40 percent considering or practicing such relationships. Some Americans, and others, choose forms of domestic organization outside married monogamy. Both queer and feminist activists and scholars have suggested that polygamy need not be as fearsome, or as oppressive to women, as it has historically been. They imagine different relationship possibilities, ones strongly allied with sex-positive, queer, and feminist realignments of domestic and sexual lives. Such activists have seen monogamous marriage as a repressive institution; they are reimagining domestic life in new ways.

Some of these forms of nonmonogamy include polyamory, with a considerable array of configurations of gender and sexual orientation. There is a great diversity of practices among those who live versions of polyamory. That is the point, after all: that one size, monogamy, does not fit all. There is often a deliberate rejection of hierarchy, or the notion that there is a first or primary partner and then secondary or somehow lesser ones. Some poly configurations involve more traditional arrangements, such as a man with more than one female partner, but there are plenty of others. Sometimes the various lovers of a person, their metamours, meet up, but sometimes they do not. In some cases, all the lovers are sexually involved with each other. In other cases, there is an anchor or nesting partner, who has a cohabiting partner and other lovers in addition, whether in the short or in the long term. Polyamorists celebrate compersion, essentially the opposite of jealousy, finding joy in a lover's enjoyment of another. Some even espouse what they call radical relationship anarchy, refusing monogamy and most other traditional arrangements.

This trend toward polyamory advocacy has its roots in twentieth-century countercultures of the 1960s and 1970s. Polyamory was part of a general questioning and utopianism, stemming from communal cultures and the impetus of the so-called sexual revolution. Such radicalism flourished on the American West Coast, in California and Oregon. One early iteration was the founding of *Loving More Magazine* (now website) by Ryam Nearing and Deborah Anapol in 1994 (though this publication had begun life in 1984 as a newsletter published by Nearing). The internet has driven this movement, with websites and podcasts providing solidarity for polyamorists as well as information and guidance for those new to the practice, in podcasts such as *Polyamory Weekly*, founded in 2005 by Cunning Minx, and *Multiamory*, a podcast about group relationships.

Although numbers are difficult to come by, it is clear that polyamory is increasingly an option in the American domestic landscape. All these relations exist despite no legal recognition for any poly arrangements and very little sense that there will be significant legal changes anytime soon, despite propolygamy legal treatises. These kinds of poly arrangements are becoming more, not less, common, especially among younger people. These new forms allow individuals to reinvent domestic life in ways that feel for them closer to achieving principles of equality and liberty. Whether this is how such relations will work in practice in the long term remains to be seen.

Contemporary polyamorists in San Francisco are very far away from wives and husbands living the Principle in Hildale. Yet all of these relationships suggest ways of navigating the pressures of modern society and monogamy. Some use polygamy to retreat from the exigencies of the modern world; for others, polyamory is a way to embrace them and to reinvent the world through domestic relationships. Polygamy can be conservative and regressive; it can also be modern and progressive. It has often been a way to mark boundaries of belonging. Polygamy's complex history demonstrates that domestic life has long been an arena for fierce contests over the right way to organize society and politics and religion and that such remains the case in the early twenty-first century.

References

Introduction

Reynolds v. United States, 98 U.S. 145 (1879). https://supreme.justia
.com/cases/federal/us/98/145/case.html.
Miriam Koktvedgaard Zeitzen, *Polygamy: A Cross-Cultural Analysis*
(Oxford: Berg, 2008), 17.

Chapter 1: Origins and overview

Bernabé Cobo, *History of the Inca Empire: An Account of the Indians'
Customs and Their Origin, Together with a Treatise on Inca
Legends, History, and Social Institutions*, trans. Roland Hamilton,
2 vols. (Austin: University of Texas Press, 1979), 1:30, 2:237.
Irene Silverblatt, *Moon, Sun, and Witches: Gender Ideologies and
Class in Inca and Colonial Peru* (Princeton, NJ: Princeton
University Press, 1987), 100.
Tamara Loos, *Subject Siam: Family, Law, and Colonial Modernity in
Thailand* (Ithaca, NY: Cornell University Press, 2006), 113, 114.
Barbara Watson Andaya, "Women and the Performance of Power in
Early Modern Southeast Asia," in *Servants of the Dynasty: Palace
Women in World History*, ed. Anne Walthall (Berkeley: University
of California Press, 2008), 29.
Keith McMahon, "The Institution of Polygamy in the Chinese Imperial
Palace," *Journal of Asian Studies* 72, no. 4 (November 2013):
921, 925–6.
Beverly Bossler, "Gender and Entertainment at the Song Court," in
Servants of the Dynasty: Palace Women in World History, ed. Anne
Walthall (Berkeley: University of California Press, 2008), 262.

Nakanyike B. Musisi, "Women, 'Elite Polygyny,' and Buganda State Formation," *Signs* 16 (1991): 777–79.

William Strachey, *The First Booke of the First Decade Contayning the Historie of Travaile into Virginia Britania*, Ashmole MS 1758, Bodleian Library, Oxford University, 60–62.

Benjamin Danks, "Marriage Customs of the New Britain Group," *Journal of the Anthropological Institute of Great Britain and Ireland* 18 (1889): 284, 293.

William Colenso, "On the Maori Races of New Zealand," *Transactions and Proceedings of the New Zealand Institute* 1 (1868): 19.

Brooke Scelza and Rebecca Bliege Bird, "Group Structure and Female Cooperative Networks in Australia's Western Desert," *Human Nature* 19 (2008): 244.

Erin T. Dailey, *Queens, Consorts, Concubines: Gregory of Tours and Women of the Merovingian Elite* (Leiden: Brill, 2015), 102.

Bart Jaski, "Marriage Laws in Ireland and on the Continent in the Early Middle Ages," in *"The Fragility of Her Sex"?: Medieval Irishwomen in Their European Context*, ed. Christine Meek and Katharine Simms (Dublin: Four Courts Press, 1996), 35–41.

Chapter 2: Monotheism

Leslie Peirce, *Empress of the East: How a Slave Girl Became Queen of the Ottoman Empire* (London: Icon Books, 2018), 41, 47–48, 59–60, 109, 159.

Mordechai Friedman, "Polygyny in Jewish Tradition and Practice: New Sources from the Cairo Geniza," *Proceedings of the American Academy for Jewish Research* 49 (1982): 36, 57.

Cairo Genizah Collection, Cambridge University Library, T-S 16.214; T-S 8.199; and T-S 20.160, accessed October 20, 2020, https://cudl.lib.cam.ac.uk/collections/genizah/1.

John Witte Jr., *The Western Case for Monogamy over Polygamy* (Cambridge: Cambridge University Press, 2015), 52–53, 59–60, 86, 90, 102–3.

Peter Biller, *The Measure of Multitude: Population in Medieval Thought* (Oxford: Oxford University Press, 2003), 84, 83–84, 71.

James Muldoon, "European Family Law and the People of the Frontier," in *Religion, Gender, and Culture in the Pre-Modern World*, ed. Alexandra Cuffel and Brian Britt (London: Palgrave Macmillan, 2007), 257.

Reuven Firestone, *Journeys into Holy Lands: The Evolution of the Abraham-Ishmael Legends in Islamic Exegesis* (Albany: State University of New York Press, 1990), 67.

Judith E. Tucker, *Women, Family, and Gender in Islamic Law* (Cambridge: Cambridge University Press, 2008), 56.

Yossef Rapoport, "Ibn Ḥajar Al-ʿasqalānī, His Wife, Her Slave-Girl: Romantic Triangles and Polygamy in Fifteenth-Century Cairo," *Annales Islamologiques* 47 (2013): 337–38.

Yossef Rapoport, "Divorce and the Elite Household in Late Medieval Cairo," *Continuity and Change* 6, no. 2 (2001): 202, 212.

Judith E. Tucker, "Marriage and Family in Nablus, 1720–1856: Toward a History of Arab Marriage," *Journal of Family History* 13, no. 2 (1988): 175.

Chapter 3: Early modern encounters

Muzaffar Alam and Sanjay Subrahmanyam, "Frank Disputations: Catholics and Muslims in the Court of Jahangir (1608–11)," *Indian Economic and Social History Review* 46, no. 4 (2009): 458, 480–82.

Domingo de San Antón Muñón Chimalpahin Quauhtlehuanitzin, *Codex Chimalpahin: Society and Politics in Mexico Tenochtitlan, Tlatelolco, Texcoco, Culhuancan, and Other Nahua Altepetl in Central Mexico*, trans. and ed. Arthur J. O. Anderson and Susan Schroeder, 2 vols. (Norman: University of Oklahoma Press, 1997), 1:149, 163, 2:83–85, 109.

Pete Sigal, *The Flower and the Scorpion: Sexuality and Ritual in Early Nahua Culture* (Durham, NC: Duke University Press, 2011), 72–73.

Susan Toby Evans, "Concubines and Cloth: Women and Weaving in Aztec Palaces and Colonial Mexico," in *Servants of the Dynasty: Palace Women in World History*, ed. Anne Walthall (Berkeley: University of California Press, 2008), 202, 218–19, 225–27.

Camilla Townsend, *Fifth Sun: A New History of the Aztecs* (Oxford: Oxford University Press, 2019), 43.

Patricia Lopes Don, "The 1539 Inquisition and Trial of Don Carlos of Texcoco in Early Mexico," *Hispanic American Historical Review* 88, no. 4 (2008): 590, 594.

Jorge Flores, *The Mughal Padshah: A Jesuit Treatise on Emperor Jahangir's Court and Household* (Leiden: Brill, 2016), 95–96.

Ruby Lal, *Empress: The Astonishing Reign of Nur Jahan* (New York: W. W. Norton, 2018), 41–42, 97, 114, 130, 139.

Ruby Lal, *Domesticity and Power in the Early Mughal World* (Cambridge: Cambridge University Press, 2005), 40.

Rosalind O'Hanlon, "Kingdom, Household and Body History, Gender and Imperial Service under Akbar," *Modern Asian Studies* 41, no. 5 (2007): 915.

Ali Anooshahr, "The King Who Would Be Man: The Gender Roles of the Warrior King in Early Mughal History," *Journal of the Royal Asiatic Society* 18, no. 3 (2008): 336.

Archibald Dalzel, *The History of Dahomy, an Inland Kingdom of Africa* (London: T. Spilsbury and Son, 1793), 129.

Chapter 4: Protestantism

Hermann von Kerssenbrock, *Narrative of the Anabaptist Madness: The Overthrow of Münster, the Famous Metropolis of Westphalia*, ed. and trans. Christopher S. Mackay, 2 vols. (Leiden: Brill, 2007), 2:567, 576, 580–82, 641.

Leo Miller, *John Milton among the Polygamophiles* (New York: Loewenthal Press, 1974), 23.

Bernardo Ochino, *A Dialogue of Polygamy* (London: John Garfield, 1657), 66.

John Weemes, *An Exposition of the Morall Law, or Ten Commandements of Almightie God, Set Downe by Way of Exercitations* (London: T. Cotes, 1632), 173.

John Milton, *The Complete Works of John Milton*. Vol. 8, *De Doctrina Christiana*, ed. John K. Hale and J. Donald Cullington (Oxford: Oxford University Press, 2012), 377–99.

Patrick Delaney, *Reflections upon Polygamy* (London: J. Roberts, 1737), 1, 22, 30, 32–33.

Martin Madan, *Thelyphthora, or, a Treatise on Female Ruin*, 2 vols. (London: J. Dodsley, 1780), 1:vii–viii, 182–84, 295–99; 2:186–96.

Polygamy, or Mahomet the Prophet to Madan the Evangelist, an Heroic Poem (London: 1782?), 71, 79.

"A Traveller," "To the Editor of the Morning Post: Polygamy," *Morning Post and Daily Advertiser* (London), November 21, 1780.

Ephraim Stinchfield, *Cochranism Delineated, or, a Description of, and a Specific for Religious Hydrophobia* (Portland: Maine Historical Society, 1819), accessed July 3, 2020, https://www.mainememory.net/artifact/13109.

Polygamy

Chapter 5: Mormonism

"Woman's Expectations" and "News and Views," *Woman's Exponent* (Salt Lake City, UT), July 1, 1877, and June 1, 1872.

Merina Smith, *Revelation, Resistance, and Mormon Polygamy: The Introduction and Implementation of the Principle, 1830–1853* (Logan: Utah State University Press, 2013), 206.

Orson Pratt as quoted in B. Carmon Hardy, ed. *Doing the Works of Abraham: Mormon Polygamy: Its Origin, Practice, and Demise* (Norman, OK: Arthur H. Clark, 2007), 87.

Kathryn M. Daynes, *"More Wives Than One": Transformation of the Mormon Marriage System, 1840–1910* (Urbana: University of Illinois Press, 2001), 72–74, 154, 196.

Paula Kelly Harline, *The Polygamous Wives Writing Club: From the Diaries of Mormon Pioneer Women* (New York: Oxford University Press, 2014), 45, 116.

Belinda Marden Pratt, *Defence of Polygamy, by a Lady of Utah* (Salt Lake City, UT: 1854).

William Chandless, *A Visit to Salt Lake* (London: Smith, Elder, 1857), 192.

J. W. Gunnison, *The Mormons, or, Latter-Day Saints* (Philadelphia: Lippincott, Grambo, 1852), 72.

Laurel Thatcher Ulrich, *A House Full of Females: Plural Marriage and Women's Rights in Early Mormonism, 1830–1870* (New York: Knopf, 2017), 156.

Annie Laurie, "First Senator among Women: Annie Laurie Interviews Martha Hughes Cannon of Utah," *San Francisco Examiner*, November 9, 1896, 63, no. 131, 1/1–2, 2/5.

Sarah Barringer Gordon, *The Mormon Question: Polygamy and Constitutional Conflict in Nineteenth-Century America* (Chapel Hill: University of North Carolina Press, 2002), 32.

Benjamin G. Ferris, *Utah and the Mormons: The History, Government, Doctrines, Customs, and Prospects of the Latter-Day Saints* (New York: Harper & Brothers, 1854), 247.

Ann Eliza Young, *Wife Number 19, or the Story of a Life in Bondage* (Hartford, CT: Dustin, Gilman, 1876), 591.

Roberts Barthelow as quoted in Samuel A. Cartwright, "Hereditary Descent; or, Depravity of the Offspring of Polygamy among the Mormons," *Debow's Review* 30, no. 2 (1861): 206.

Francis Lieber, "Shall Utah Be Admitted to the Union?" *Putnam's Monthly Magazine of American Literature, Science, and Art* 5, no. 27 (March 1855): 234.

Reynolds v. United States, 98 U.S. 145 (1879), https://supreme.justia
.com/cases/federal/us/98/145/case.html.

Richard S. Van Wagoner, *Mormon Polygamy: A History*, 2nd ed. (Salt
Lake City, UT: Signature Books, 1989), 26, 99.

Chapter 6: Modern encounters

Seniha Sultan as quoted in Nilüfer Göle, *The Forbidden Modern:
Civilization and Veiling* (Ann Arbor: University of Michigan Press,
2013), 27; also 33, 75.

Mary Wollstonecraft, *A Vindication of the Rights of Woman* (London:
J. Johnson, 1792), 79.

Melek-Hanum, wife of H. H. Kibrizli-Mehemet-Pasha, *Thirty Years in
the Harem* (London: Chapman and Hall, 1872), 161.

Lisa Pollard, *Nurturing the Nation: The Family Politics of Modernizing,
Colonizing, and Liberating Egypt, 1805–1923* (Berkeley: University
of California Press, 2005), 68–69, 93, 96.

Kenneth M. Cuno, *Modernizing Marriage: Family, Ideology, and Law
in Nineteenth- and Early Twentieth-Century Egypt* (Syracuse, NY:
Syracuse University Press, 2015), 43, 120.

Qasim Amin, *The Liberation of Women and the New Woman: Two
Documents in the History of Egyptian Feminism*, ed. and trans.
Saika Sidhom Peterson (Cairo: American University in Cairo Press,
2000), 84–86.

George W. Gawrych, "Şemseddin Sami, Women, and Social
Conscience in the Late Ottoman Empire," *Middle Eastern Studies*
46, no. 1 (2010): 103.

Anna H. Leonowens, *The Romance of the Harem* (Boston: James
R. Osgood, 1873), 44, 107.

Matthew H. Sommer, *Polyandry and Wife-Selling in Qing Dynasty
China: Survival Strategies and Judicial Interventions* (Berkeley:
University of California Press, 2015), 29.

Mary Eliza Tracy Allred as quoted in B. Carmon Hardy, ed. *Doing the
Works of Abraham: Mormon Polygamy: Its Origin, Practice, and
Demise*, vol. 9, *Kingdom in the West: The Mormons and the
American Frontier* (Norman, OK: Arthur H. Clark, 2007), 173.

Sarah Carter, *The Importance of Being Monogamous: Marriage and
Nation Building in Western Canada to 1915* (Edmonton:
University of Alberta Press, 2008), 44–48, 53, 88, 115, 198–99,
212, 219.

Dan Erickson, "Alberta Polygamists? The Canadian Climate and Response to the Introduction of Mormonism's 'Peculiar Institution,'" *Pacific Northwest Quarterly* 86, no. 4 (1995): 158.

Beverly Hungry Wolf, *The Ways of My Grandmothers* (New York: William Morrow, 1980), 146.

Nan Seuffert, "Shaping the Modern Nation: Colonial Marriage Law, Polygamy and Concubinage in Aotearoa New Zealand," *Law Text Culture* 7 (2003): 196, 211–12.

Chapter 7: Contemporary debates

Mana A. Z. Yamani, *Polygamy and Law in Contemporary Saudi Arabia* (Reading, UK: Ithaca Press, 2008), 23–24, 186, 188.

Judith E. Tucker, *Women, Family, and Gender in Islamic Law* (Cambridge: Cambridge University Press, 2008), 77.

Kgaugelo Masweneng, "More 'Empowering' to Be a Second Wife," March 6, 2017, Sowetan Live, https://www.sowetanlive.co.za/news/2017-03-06-more-empowering-to-be-a-second-wife/.

Martha Bradley-Evans, *Kidnapped from That Land: The Government Raids on the Short Creek Polygamists* (Salt Lake City: University of Utah Press, 1993), 104.

Lisa A. Mazzie, "Dissent in Obergefell v. Hodges," *Marquette University Law School* (blog), July 8, 2015, https://law.marquette.edu/facultyblog/2015/07/the-initial-appeal-of-chief-justice-john-roberts-dissent-in-obergefell-v-hodges/comment-page-1/.

Jamie Ballard, "One-Third of Americans Say Their Ideal Relationship Is Non-monogamous," YouGov America, January 31, 2020, https://today.yougov.com/topics/relationships/articles-reports/2020/01/31/millennials-monogamy-poly-poll-survey-data.

Further reading

Origins and overview

Bennion, Janet, and Lisa Fishbayn Joffe, eds. *The Polygamy Question*. Logan: Utah State University Press, 2016.

Cott, Nancy F. *Public Vows: A History of Marriage and the Nation*. Cambridge, MA: Harvard University Press, 2000.

Karras, Ruth. *Unmarriages: Women, Men, and Sexual Unions in the Middle Ages*. Philadelphia: University of Pennsylvania Press, 2012.

Loos, Tamara. *Subject Siam: Family, Law, and Colonial Modernity in Thailand*. Ithaca, NY: Cornell University Press, 2006.

Pearsall, Sarah M. S. *Polygamy: An Early American History*. New Haven, CT: Yale University Press, 2019.

Plane, Ann Marie. *Colonial Intimacies: Indian Marriage in Early New England*. Ithaca, NY: Cornell University Press, 2000.

Samson, Jane. *Race and Redemption: British Missionaries Encounter Pacific Peoples, 1797–1920*. Grand Rapids, MI: Eerdmans, 2017.

Scelza, Brooke, and Rebecca Bliege Bird. "Group Structure and Female Cooperative Networks in Australia's Western Desert." *Human Nature* 19 (2008): 231–48.

Silverblatt, Irene. *Moon, Sun, and Witches: Gender Ideologies and Class in Inca and Colonial Peru*. Princeton, NJ: Princeton University Press, 1987.

Townsend, Camilla. *Pocahontas and the Powhatan Dilemma*. New York: Hill & Wang, 2004.

Walthall, Anne, ed. *Servants of the Dynasty: Palace Women in World History*. Berkeley: University of California Press, 2008.

Zeitzen, Miriam Koktvedgaard. *Polygamy: A Cross-Cultural Analysis*. Oxford: Berg, 2008.

Monotheism

Barlas, Asma. *Believing Women in Islam: Unreading Patriarchal Interpretations of the Qu'ran.* 2nd ed. Austin: University of Texas Press, 2019.

Feller, Bruce. *Abraham: A Journey into the Heart of Three Faiths.* New York: Harper Perennial, 2002.

McDougall, Sara. *Bigamy and Christian Identity in Late Medieval Champagne.* Philadelphia: University of Pennsylvania Press, 2012.

Peirce, Leslie. *Empress of the East: How a Slave Girl Became Queen of the Ottoman Empire.* London: Icon Books, 2018.

Peirce, Leslie P. *The Imperial Harem: Women and Sovereignty in the Ottoman Empire.* New York: Oxford University Press, 1993.

Tucker, Judith E. *In the House of the Law: Gender and Islamic Law in Ottoman Syria and Palestine.* Berkeley: University of California Press, 1998.

Wadud, Amina. *Qu'ran and Woman: Rereading the Sacred Text from a Woman's Perspective.* Oxford: Oxford University Press, 1999.

Witte, John, Jr. *The Western Case for Monogamy over Polygamy.* Cambridge Studies in Law and Christianity. Edited by John Witte Jr. Cambridge: Cambridge University Press, 2015.

Early modern encounters

Balabanlilar, Lisa. *The Emperor Jahangir: Power and Kingship in Mughal India.* London: I. B. Tauris, 2020.

Bay, Edna G. *Wives of the Leopard: Gender, Politics, and Culture in the Kingdom of Dahomey.* Charlottesville: University of Virginia Press, 1998.

Hassig, Ross. *Polygamy and the Rise and Demise of the Aztec Empire.* Albuquerque: University of New Mexico Press, 2016.

Hilton, Anne. *The Kingdom of Kongo.* Oxford: Clarendon Press, 1985.

Lal, Ruby. *Domesticity and Power in the Early Mughal World.* Cambridge Studies in Islamic Civilization. Cambridge: Cambridge University Press, 2005.

Lal, Ruby. *Empress: The Astonishing Reign of Nur Jahan.* New York: W. W. Norton, 2018.

Sigal, Pete. *The Flower and the Scorpion: Sexuality and Ritual in Early Nahua Culture.* Durham, NC: Duke University Press, 2011.

Townsend, Camilla. *Fifth Sun: A New History of the Aztecs.* New York: Oxford University Press, 2019.

Protestantism

Cairncross, John. *After Polygamy Was Made a Sin: The Social History of Christian Polygamy*. London: Routledge, 1974.

Foster, Lawrence. *Religion and Sexuality: The Shakers, the Mormons, and the Oneida Community*. Urbana: University of Illinois Press, 1984.

Miller, Leo. *John Milton among the Polygamophiles*. New York: Loewenthal Press, 1974.

Miller, Nicholas B. *John Millar and the Scottish Enlightenment: Family Life and World History*. Oxford: Oxford University Press, 2017.

Roper, Lyndal. *The Holy Household: Women and Morals in Reformation Augsburg*. Oxford: Clarendon Press, 1989.

Mormonism

Daynes, Kathryn M. *"More Wives Than One": Transformation of the Mormon Marriage System, 1840–1910*. Urbana: University of Illinois Press, 2001.

Gordon, Sarah Barringer. *The Mormon Question: Polygamy and Constitutional Conflict in Nineteenth-Century America*. Chapel Hill: University of North Carolina Press, 2002.

Hardy, B. Carmon, ed. *Doing the Works of Abraham: Mormon Polygamy: Its Origin, Practice, and Demise*. Vol. 9 of *Kingdom in the West: The Mormons and the American Frontier*, edited by Will Bagley. Norman, OK: Arthur H. Clark, 2007.

Harline, Paula Kelly. *The Polygamous Wives Writing Club: From the Diaries of Mormon Pioneer Women*. New York: Oxford University Press, 2014.

Park, Benjamin E. *Kingdom of Nauvoo: The Rise and Fall of a Religious Empire on the American Frontier*. New York: Liveright/Norton, 2020.

Reeve, W. Paul. *Religion of a Different Color: Race and the Mormon Struggle for Whiteness*. New York: Oxford University Press, 2015.

Talbot, Christine. *A Foreign Kingdom: Mormons and Polygamy in American Political Culture, 1852–1890*. Urbana: University of Illinois Press, 2013.

Ulrich, Laurel Thatcher. *A House Full of Females: Plural Marriage and Women's Rights in Early Mormonism, 1830–1870*. New York: Knopf, 2017.

Van Wagoner, Richard S. *Mormon Polygamy: A History*. 2nd ed. Salt Lake City, UT: Signature Books, 1989.

Modern encounters

Booth, Marilyn. "Before Qasim Amin: Writing Histories of Gender Politics in 1890s Egypt." In *The Long 1890s in Egypt: Colonial Quiescence, Subterranean Resistance*, edited by Marilyn Booth and Anthony Gorman, 365–98. Edinburgh: Edinburgh University Press, 2014.

Carter, Sarah. *The Importance of Being Monogamous: Marriage and Nation Building in Western Canada to 1915*. Edmonton: University of Alberta Press, 2008.

Cuno, Kenneth M. *Modernizing Marriage: Family, Ideology, and Law in Nineteenth- and Early Twentieth-Century Egypt*. Syracuse, NY: Syracuse University Press, 2015.

McDannell, Colleen. *Sister Saints: Mormon Women since the End of Polygamy*. New York: Oxford University Press, 2019.

McGrath, Ann. *Illicit Love: Interracial Sex and Marriage in the United States and Australia*. Lincoln: University of Nebraska Press, 2015.

Nast, Heidi J. *Concubines and Power: Five Hundred Years in a Northern Nigerian Palace*. Minneapolis: University of Minnesota Press, 2004.

Pollard, Lisa. *Nurturing the Nation: The Family Politics of Modernizing, Colonizing, and Liberating Egypt, 1805–1923*. Berkeley: University of California Press, 2005.

Seuffert, Nan. *Jurisprudence of National Identity: Kaleidoscopes of Imperialism and Globalisation from Aotearoa New Zealand*. Aldershot, Hampshire: Ashgate, 2006.

Sommer, Matthew H. *Polyandry and Wife-Selling in Qing Dynasty China: Survival Strategies and Judicial Interventions*. Berkeley: University of California Press, 2015.

Contemporary debates

Anapol, Deborah. *Polyamory in the Twenty-First Century: Love and Intimacy with Multiple Partners*. Lanham, MD: Rowman & Littlefield, 2012.

Bailey, Martha, and Amy J. Kaufman. *Polygamy in the Monogamous World: Multicultural Challenges for Western Law and Policy*. Santa Barbara, CA: Praeger, 2010.

Bennion, Janet. *Polygamy in Primetime: Media, Gender, and Politics in Mormon Fundamentalism.* Waltham. MA: Brandeis University Press, 2012.

Bennion, Janet. *Women of Principle: Female Networking in Contemporary Mormon Polygyny.* New York: Oxford University Press, 1998.

Bradley-Evans, Martha. *Kidnapped from That Land: The Government Raids on the Short Creek Polygamists.* Salt Lake City: University of Utah Press, 1993.

Goldfeder, Mark. *Legalizing Plural Marriage: The Next Frontier in Family Law.* Waltham, MA: Brandeis University Press, 2017.

Jessop, Carolyn, with Laura Palmer. *Escape.* New York: Broadway Books, 2007.

Otter, Ronald C. Den. *In Defense of Plural Marriage.* Cambridge: Cambridge University Press, 2015.

Tucker, Judith E. *Women, Family, and Gender in Islamic Law.* Cambridge: Cambridge University Press, 2008.

Zeitzen, Miriam Koktvedgaard. "The Many Wives of Jacob Zuma." *Foreign Policy*, March 11, 2010. https://foreignpolicy.com/2010/03/11/the-many-wives-of-jacob-zuma/.

Index

Index

SEXUALITY
A Very Short Introduction
Veronique Mottier

What shapes our sexuality? Is it a product of our genes, or of society, culture, and politics? How have concepts of sexuality and sexual norms changed over time? How have feminist theories, religion, and HIV/AIDS affected our attitudes to sex? Focusing on the social, political, and psychological aspects of sexuality, this *Very Short Introduction* examines these questions and many more, exploring what shapes our sexuality, and how our attitudes to sex have in turn shaped the wider world. Revealing how our assumptions about what is 'normal' in sexuality have, in reality, varied widely across time and place, this book tackles the major topics and controversies that still confront us when issues of sex and sexuality are discussed: from sex education, HIV/AIDS, and eugenics, to religious doctrine, gay rights, and feminism.

www.oup.com/vsi

WITCHCRAFT
A Very Short Introduction
Malcolm Gaskill

Witchcraft is a subject that fascinates us all, and everyone knows
what a witch is - or do they? From childhood most of us develop a
sense of the mysterious, malign person, usually an old woman.
Historically, too, we recognize witch-hunting as a feature of pre-
modern societies. But why do witches still feature so heavily in our
cultures and consciousness? From Halloween to superstitions,
and literary references such as Faust and even Harry Potter,
witches still feature heavily in our society. In this Very Short
Introduction Malcolm Gaskill challenges all of this, and argues
that what we think we know is, in fact, wrong.

'Each chapter in this small but perfectly-formed book could be the
jumping-off point for a year's stimulating reading. Buy it now.'

Fortean Times

CHRISTIAN ETHICS
A Very Short Introduction
D. Stephen Long

This *Very Short Introduction* to Christian ethics introduces the topic by examining its sources and historical basis. D. Stephen Long presents a discussion of the relationship between Christian ethics, modern, and postmodern ethics, and explores practical issues including sex, money, and power. Long recognises the inherent difficulties in bringing together 'Christian' and 'ethics' but argues that this is an important task for both the Christian faith and for ethics. Arguing that Christian ethics are not a precise science, but the cultivation of practical wisdom from a range of sources, Long also discusses some of the failures of the Christian tradition, including the crusades, the conquest, slavery, inquisitions, and the Galileo affair.

www.oup.com/vsi

FASHION
A Very Short Introduction
Rebecca Arnold

Fashion is a dynamic global industry that plays an important role
in the economic, political, cultural, and social lives of an
international audience. It spans high art and popular culture, and
plays a significant role in material and visual culture. This book
introduces fashion's myriad influences and manifestations.
Fashion is explored as a creative force, a business, and a means
of communication. From Karl Lagerfeld's creative reinventions of
Chanel's iconic style to the multicultural reference points of Indian
designer Manish Arora, from the spectacular fashion shows held
in nineteenth century department stores to the mix-and-match
styles of Japanese youth, the book examines the ways that
fashion both reflects and shapes contemporary culture.

'Her fascinating little book makes a good framework for
independent study and has a very useful bibliography.'

Philippa Stockley, Times Literary Supplement

BEAUTY
A Very Short Introduction
Roger Scruton

In this *Very Short Introduction* the renowned philosopher Roger
Scruton explores the concept of beauty, asking what makes an
object - either in art, in nature, or the human form - beautiful,
and examining how we can compare differing judgements of
beauty when it is evident all around us that our tastes vary so
widely. Is there a right judgement to be made about beauty?
Is it right to say there is more beauty in a classical temple than
a concrete office block, more in a Rembrandt than in last year's
Turner Prize winner? Forthright and thought-provoking, and as
accessible as it is intellectually rigorous, this introduction to the
philosophy of beauty draws conclusions that some may find
controversial, but, as Scruton shows, help us to find greater
sense of meaning in the beautiful objects that fill our lives.

A fascinating book, which I heartily recommend.

Brya Wilson, Readers Digest